ASTD Training Basics Series

ORGANIZATION DEVELOPMENT *Basics*

LISA HANEBERG

A Complete, How-to Guide to Help You:

 Understand and Use Core OD Principles

 Improve How People and Processes Perform

 Use Your Knowledge to Meet Organizational Goals

ATD Press is an internationally renowned source of insightful and practical information on talent development, training, and professional development.

ATD Press
1640 King Street
Alexandria, VA 22314 USA

Ordering information: Books published by ATD Press can be purchased by visiting ATD's website at www.td.org/books or by calling 800.628.2783 or 703.683.8100.

Library of Congress Control Number: 2005922087

ISBN-10: 1-56286-411-4
ISBN-13: 978-1-56286-411-8
e-ISBN: 978-1-60728-465-9

Editorial Staff
Acquisitions and Development Editor: Mark Morrow
Copyeditor: April Davis
Interior Design and Production: Kathleen Schaner
Cover Design: Kristi Sone
Cover Illustration: Michael Aveto

Printed by BR Printers, San Jose, CA

Table of Contents

About the
Training Basics Series

■■■■■■■■■■■■■■■■■■■■■■■■■■■■■■■■■■■■■■

ASTD's *Training Basics* series recognizes and, in some ways, celebrates the fast-paced, ever-changing reality of organizations today. Jobs, roles, and expectations change quickly. One day you might be a network administrator or a process line manager, and the next day you might be asked to train 50 employees in basic computer skills or to instruct line workers in quality processes.

Where do you turn for help? The ASTD *Training Basics* series is designed to be your one-stop solution. The series takes a minimalist approach to your learning curve dilemma and presents only the information you need to be successful. Each book in the series guides you through key aspects of training: giving presentations, making the transition to the role of trainer, designing and delivering training, and evaluating training. The books in the series also include some advanced skills such as performance and basic business proficiencies.

The ASTD *Training Basics* series is the perfect tool for training and performance professionals looking for easy-to-understand materials that will prepare non-trainers to take on a training role. In addition, this series is the perfect reference tool for any trainer's bookshelf and a quick way to hone your existing skills. The titles currently planned for the series include:

- ▶ *Presentation Basics* (2003)
- ▶ *Trainer Basics* (2003)
- ▶ *Training Design Basics* (2003)
- ▶ *Facilitation Basics* (2004)
- ▶ *Communication Basics* (2004)
- ▶ *Performance Basics* (2004)
- ▶ *Evaluation Basics* (2005)
- ▶ *Needs Assessment Basics* (2005)
- ▶ *ROI Basics* (2005)
- ▶ *Organization Development Basics* (2005).

Preface

■ ■

The field of organization development (OD) exists to enable people and organizations to do their best work. It's a growing and important discipline. As a company's requirements to compete and improve efficiency increase, so too does its need for effective OD. *Organization Development Basics* is a primer on common OD practices and introduces several methods within the field.

What Is Organization Development?

Organization development work is, at its core, a purposeful and systemic body of work that improves how people and processes perform. Activities and initiatives represent a conscious and planned process to align the various aspects of the organization to meet its goals. Organization development professionals seek to improve the organization's capabilities as measured by its efficiency, effectiveness, health, culture, and business results. They do this by facilitating, consulting, coaching, analyzing, training, and designing.

There is some disagreement within the field about which practices and tools fit in OD. Some adopt a narrow interpretation that focuses on organization alignment and change intervention. Others see OD as a broader set of practices that includes leadership, diversity, and team training. There is some overlap of skills and practices among OD, training, human resources, project management, and quality improvement. To muddy the definition further, each company interprets these functional boundaries differently.

According to the Organization Development Network, a professional organization for OD practitioners, "Organization Development is a values-based approach to systems change in organizations and communities; it strives to build the capacity to achieve and sustain a new desired state that benefits the organization or community and the world around them."

Warner Burke, an OD pioneer, said, "Most people in the field agree that OD involves consultants who try to help clients improve their organizations by applying knowledge from the behavior sciences—psychology, sociology, cultural anthropology, and certain related disciplines. Most would also agree that OD implies change and, if we accept that improvement in organizational functioning means that change has occurred, then, broadly defined, OD means organizational change."

These two definitions share the notion that OD focuses on helping an organization get from Point A to Point B using a systemic approach based on knowledge of the behavioral sciences. The definitions also emphasize that OD work involves managing and implementing change. *Organization Development Basics* presents a broad view of OD and touches on a long list of practices and disciplines. Based on actual OD job descriptions, the systemic approach is consistent with the requirements of most OD positions because companies are looking for OD professionals who can perform an abundance of tasks. That said, there are fundamental practices required of most OD practitioners, such as consulting, facilitating, coaching, analyzing, and managing change. This book delves into these and other fundamental OD practices and will briefly mention other methods.

Who Should Read This Book?

This book is a primer on the broad field of OD, and will serve several audiences:

- ▶ Trainers who want to learn more about OD and add to their list of capabilities
- ▶ Managers who want to learn basic OD techniques to improve team performance and satisfaction
- ▶ Organization development professionals at the beginning of their careers
- ▶ Human resources professionals.

Organization Development Basics offers just the right amount of information to create an understanding of the tools, practices, and core skills of OD. Readers can use the book's suggestions to apply basic OD techniques.

Look for These Icons

This book strives to make it easy for you to understand and apply its lessons. Icons throughout this book help you identify key points.

What's Inside This Chapter

Each chapter opens with a summary of the topics addressed in the chapter. You can use this reference to find the areas that interest you most.

Think About This

These are helpful tips for how to use the tools and techniques presented in the chapter.

Basic Rules

These rules cut to the chase. They represent important concepts and assumptions that form the foundation of OD.

Noted

This icon calls out additional information.

Getting It Done

The final section of each chapter supports your ability to apply OD tools and techniques. This section offers suggestions, additional resources, or questions that will help you get started.

Acknowledgments

This book represents a culmination of my 20-year (and counting) exploration into the world of OD. I have enjoyed the advice and coaching of many talented folks along the way and would like to thank them. Thanks to Dave Borden, Jim Booth, Peter Capezio, Bob Drinane, Ralph Stayer, Charlie Jacobs, Laurie Ford, Jeffrey Ford, Stephen Covey, Alfie Kohn, Ilean Galloway, Roger Schwarz, Kate Mulqueen, Linda O'Toole, and the many others who have helped shape and expand my OD practice.

Lisa Haneberg
September 2005

Organization Development's Contribution to Business Success

░░

 What's Inside This Chapter

In this chapter, you'll learn:

▶ The three components of the OD approach
▶ A set of OD values
▶ The basic elements of systems thinking
▶ Major contributions made by OD pioneers.

Organization development practitioners help companies manage change and align people, processes, and practices for success. They do this by stepping outside the concerns of a specific function (like human resources, operations, sales) and observing the inner workings of the organization. In its simplest form, OD work aims to be a catalyst that helps the organization get from where is it today (Point A) to its desired state (Point B). Figure 1-1 shows this fundamental relationship. Another way to state the purpose of OD work is to say that it helps systems get better. As

Figure 1-1. The purpose of organization development.

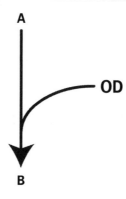

systems, organizations can get out of alignment; their parts may not connect and communication does not flow.

Organization development professionals improve the health of the system by employing various products and services. A set of values and a system orientation back up OD products and services. Methods reflect the progress behavioral sciences researchers have made in better understanding workplace dynamics. Figure 1-2 shows a more elaborate view of OD work.

Organization development professionals help organizations, teams, and individuals be more successful and effective. Progress should be faster and better. Change efforts should be more successful. The organization should be more effective and its members more engaged and satisfied. It is all possible with a strong OD function.

The Three Components of the Organization Development Approach

A distinguishing characteristic of OD work is its approach to improving organizations. The OD approach forms the basis for thought and action. There are three major components to the OD approach, as shown in figure 1-3. Organization development practitioners approach their work from a systems-thinking perspective, with a set of values about how people and organizations best work, and they use behavioral sciences theories and research to improve organization and individual success.

Figure 1-2. Organization development strengthens systems.

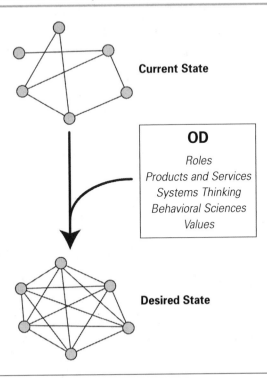

Current State

OD

Roles
Products and Services
Systems Thinking
Behavioral Sciences
Values

Desired State

Figure 1-3. The organization development approach.

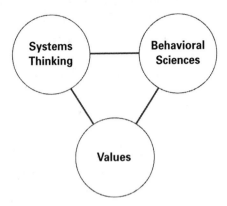

Organization Development Values

A set of common values guides OD professionals. Values are the most important component of the OD approach because they shape decisions and results.

▸ *Engagement:* With the right environment, culture, and structure, most organizations can build a successful workplace where workers feel engaged and needed.

▸ *Relationship:* Building a strong and trusting relationship is of paramount importance. Business is a social sport, and healthy relationships will facilitate success and satisfaction.

▸ *Authenticity:* Open and authentic communication is critical to the quality of business solutions and relationships. Systems that promote and reinforce authenticity enable quick problem identification and resolution.

▸ *Inclusion:* An inclusive organization brings out the best in people. Communication processes allow for participation and collaboration.

▸ *Learning Environment:* A learning environment improves self-discovery and awareness. Employees and teams discuss strengths and weaknesses and feel support when developing new skills.

▸ *Respect:* Each member of the organization adds to its value. Individuals and teams should demonstrate respect and appreciation for one another through work and decisions.

▸ *Empowerment:* Appropriate division of work and empowering others help ensure the organization realizes its capacity. When managers disempower employees, work is less intrinsically satisfying and roles are inefficient.

▸ *Flexibility:* There are many potential opportunities and solutions. Being flexible will allow for more and better creativity and collaboration.

▸ *Proactivity:* Organization development work is most effective when it is proactive versus reactive. While responding to circumstances is sometimes required, OD interventions look forward to help the organization succeed today and in the future.

These fundamental values permeate OD work. Organization development practitioners can use this list as a filter when designing initiatives and diagnosing current states.

Basic Rule 1

Values are at the core of OD practices.

Which values does your organization embody? A value is a shared belief that drives behaviors. To determine prevalent values that exist in the company, look at the collective practices and behaviors of leaders and employees. What do you see? What is your perception about what the organization values? Ask employees their perspective; the actual values are often different than the framed statements on the cafeteria wall. Using table 1-1, look for signs of the values important to OD professionals. Think about ways that you and the organization leaders can better demonstrate these values.

Table 1-1. Organization development values in action.

Value	Behavioral Evidence of This Value	Ideas for Strengthening This Value's Presence
Engagement		
Relationship		
Authenticity		
Inclusion		
Learning Environment		
Respect		
Empowerment		
Flexibility		
Proactivity		

 Think About This

Create a list of values and beliefs that you want to strengthen within the organization. Take your list with you to meetings, and when considering alternatives, assess each potential decision or approach against how well it supports the desired values. You may find that by making small changes, decisions and projects can better support values and strengthen the organization's culture and results.

Systems Thinking

Organization development practitioners strive to improve the effectiveness and capacity of the organization and its members using a systemic approach to change management and implementation. They look at the organization as a system, and parts of the organization may be smaller systems.

To understand the factors affecting results, OD practitioners consider many elements within the system:

- *Structure:* How is the work divvied up? What are people's roles? How do roles interrelate? How are roles defined from various parts of the organization?
- *Culture:* What are the shared assumptions and beliefs? How do people generally feel about working for the company? What are the automatic or learned reactions to change and innovation? Why do people leave the organization? Why do they stay with the organization? What are the unwritten values and rules of the organization?
- *Process:* Which processes influence the system's performance? How are processes evaluated and maintained? In what ways are processes enabling or getting in the way of results?
- *Practice:* How do people go about doing their work? How are practices created, communicated, and changed? Which practices are shared, and which are unique? Who decides how work will be done?
- *Goal:* What are the goals (stated and unstated) of the organization? How are goals communicated and how well are they understood? To what degree are organization goals and group goals in alignment? How well is the organization meeting its goals?
- *Organization metric:* How is success defined and measured? How do individuals and teams know whether their work is meeting the organization's goals? How and to whom are measurements communicated?

Noted

An OD practitioner is anyone who is doing OD work. Often, human resources and training professionals are also OD practitioners.

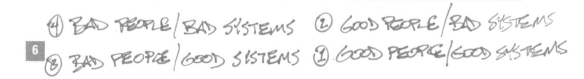

④ BAD PEOPLE/BAD SYSTEMS ② GOOD PEOPLE/BAD SYSTEMS
③ BAD PEOPLE/GOOD SYSTEMS ① GOOD PEOPLE/GOOD SYSTEMS

- *Communication and decision-making process:* How and by whom are decisions made? How easy or difficult is it to get a decision made in the organization? How are decisions and requests for decisions communicated? How does communication flow through the organization?
- *Technology:* How is technology being used? How are technology solutions enabling or getting in the way of results? How is technology maintained, improved, and explained?
- *Workflow:* What are the steps that work follows from beginning to end? Where does workflow slow or stall? How does each step serve and contribute to the final product? How is the workflow explained and updated?
- *Skill:* How are individuals and teams trained? Are there skills gaps? To meet the organization's goal, what new skills will need to be developed? How well are managers coached and developed? How do people learn what they need to know to do their jobs?
- *Management practice:* What assumptions about management determine practices and policies? How is performance managed? How do managers and senior leaders interact and communicate? How well do managers partner with each other? How do managers communicate with individuals and teams? What are the requirements (stated and real) to become a manager?

Noted

"A system is a set of interrelated elements unified by design to achieve some purpose or goal. Organizations are systems." (Harvey and Brown, An Experiential Approach to Organization Development *[1988]).*

Basic Rule 2

Organization development work is systemic and helps companies manage and implement change.

Organization development work is, by its nature, analytical. To see and understand systemic elements, OD practitioners need to assess and analyze data, observations, and feedback. To design an effective solution, they need to understand and plan for how systemic elements interrelate. Each OD initiative may include projects and tasks that address any number of systemic elements, and no two initiatives will be the same or include the same elements. Each component of an OD initiative should link to and support the other, and all parts should facilitate optimal change to the desired state. Organization development practitioners keep an eye toward the system even when performing individual tasks, such as facilitating a meeting or coaching a leader. The primary focus and objective for the OD practitioner, then, is to work with the client to assess and recommend the most appropriate response to enable the company, as a system, to progress. These responses may be comprehensive initiatives or individual projects or services.

Noted

Organization development practitioners use the term intervention *to describe a set of structured activities applied to an organization to understand and improve its results. Facilitating a one-hour meeting is not an intervention unless it is one task among several linked to a particular, desired outcome. Interventions are often needed to create lasting change.*

Organization Development's Behavioral Sciences Roots

Organization development is a discipline that was born out of the need and desire to affect organization results. Organization development uses behavioral sciences research and theories about organization change, systems, teams, and individuals. The ancestry of OD goes back to Carl Jung and Abraham Maslow, who fathered the humanistic branch of psychology, and Frederick Taylor, most known for scientific management. Early OD researchers sought to discover how the organization's underlying systems operated and changed. The first thrust of OD work began in social laboratories in the 1930s and 1940s, but quickly grew as researchers, educators, and businesses began using surveys, interviews, and studies to understand how people and systems work. Companies called upon social scientists to help them improve productivity and throughput. Here are several OD pioneers and the contributions for which they are best known:

- Kurt Lewin (1890–1947) is sometimes called the grandfather of OD because of his profound effect on the field. Many OD methods can be traced back to work done by Lewin. His work focused on experiential learning, group dynamics, force-field analysis, and action research (the foundation of most change initiatives). Lewin performed some of the earliest studies using self-managed work teams in the 1930s. Lewin is also credited with creating T-groups.

- Douglas McGregor (1906–1964) was a social psychologist who created the Theory X and Theory Y management model. This model held that Theory X managers believed that workers were lazy and greedy, and must be controlled and monitored. Theory Y managers believed that people wanted to do a good job, grow, and contribute, and needed coaching, support, and minimal direction to do their best work. McGregor's work demonstrated that to succeed, companies must cultivate an organization environment that engages and intrinsically motivates workers (Theory Y).

- Rensis Likert (1903–1981) is most recognized in association with the Likert Scale, the widely used scale for attitude measurement. A Likert Scale contains an odd number of choices (usually five or seven), anchored by two extremes, ranging from favorable to unfavorable, with a neutral midpoint. Likert's important work also includes advances in participative management theories.

- Richard Beckhard (1918–1999) was one of the first to view the corporation as a system and recognize the importance of group process. Beckhard was

Noted

T-groups are small groups of people that guide their own development and understanding by openly talking about and examining issues, concerns, beliefs, and ideas. The facilitator establishes the framework for the discussion and suggests ground rules, but otherwise lets the group take ownership for its learning process. The T-group experience can be intense and personal. Many training programs still use derivations of the T-group.

also a pioneer in organizational change theory and his work still forms the foundation for many of today's models of large-scale organizational change. Beckhard is credited as being the first person to use the term *organization development* in relation to change-process work. He launched the Organization Development Network in 1967 in partnership with the National Training Laboratory.

▸ Wilfred Bion (1897–1979) created the Tavistock Method while trying to treat British World War II soldiers. He observed and experimented with groups who could empower themselves to help each other solve problems and take responsibility for their work. Bion emphasized the importance of the leader's conduct and style to the outcome of the group's work.

▸ Ed Schein (1928–) focused his work on organizational culture, process consultation, and career dynamics. Schein is credited with pioneering methods for evaluating and shaping corporate culture.

▸ Warren Bennis (1925–) was one of the nation's foremost authorities on OD, leadership, and change. His work focused on the areas of leadership, change, and creative collaboration. Bennis was successor to Douglas McGregor as chairman of the organization studies department at MIT. Bennis wrote several leadership books that have stood the test of time and are still listed among the best-selling books in the genre.

▸ Chris Argyris (1923–) researched the relationship of people and organizations, how organizations learn, and uses of action. Many consider him the father of the learning organization. Argyris is most known for his development of the single-loop double-loop learning model (developed with Donald Schön).

The field of OD has had many important contributors, several of whom are still active today. Contemporary OD experts include David Cooperrider (Appreciative Inquiry), Peter Senge (Systems and Learning Organization), William Bridges (Change), Warner Burke (Leadership and Organization Dynamics), Chris Worley (Strategic Change), Rosabeth Moss Kanter (Change), Margaret Wheatley (Systems), Peter Block (Consulting and Empowerment), Ed Lawler (Human Resources and Organization Effectiveness), David Ulrich (Organization Change and Capability), Marshall Goldsmith (Executive Coaching), Marvin Weisbord (Future Search), Edie

Basic Rule 3

Organization development practices are backed up by behavioral sciences research and theories.

Seashore (Change Management and Conflict Resolution), Thomas Cummings (Systems Theory), David Jamieson (Leadership and Facilitation), Suresh Srivastva (Appreciative Inquiry), and Stephen Covey (Leadership and Values). Organization development is a field that has and will inspire rich debate, research, and growth.

The OD approach offers practitioners a strong foundation from which to help organizations and individuals prosper. Organization development practitioners use values, systems thinking, and behavioral sciences theories to diagnose the organization's opportunities and design appropriate interventions. The OD approach forms the basis for how organization development professionals conduct their work.

Getting It Done

In this chapter, you learned the three elements of the OD approach: values, systems thinking, and behavioral sciences theories. Exercise 1-1 allows you to apply systems thinking to an organizational opportunity.

This chapter introduced you to the elements that form the foundation of all OD work. In the next chapter, you will learn about typical OD jobs.

Exercise 1-1. Applying systems thinking.

Select a major corporate goal. (Example: Reduce the product development cycle and introduce 18 new products in three years.)

Goal: _____

For this goal, write down what needs to be considered for each systemic element. Your response can be phrased in the form of a statement or a question. For example:

> Structure: How will roles need to be changed? Cross-functional and matrixed teams might need to be created. Reporting relationships shift to product lines?

Systemic Elements	Influences This Goal By . . .
Structure	
Culture	
Process	
Practice	
Goal	
Organization metric	
Communication and decision-making process	
Technology	
Workflow	
Skill	
Management practice	

2

The Job of Organization Development

⬛ ⬛

What's Inside This Chapter

In this chapter, you'll learn:

▶ The most common OD job titles
▶ The OD services most sought by employers
▶ The core skills that OD practitioners need.

Sixty-Seven Job Descriptions

Organization development practitioners hold a variety of jobs, many that overlap with the disciplines of training and human resources. An analysis of OD job descriptions was conducted to understand the breadth of OD titles and responsibilities. Over a 24-hour period, OD job descriptions were collected from Internet job sites, including the OD Network Website, Society for Human Resource Management Website, ASTD Website, Monster.com, Careerbuilder.com, and Hotjobs.com. In this 24-hour period, 67 job descriptions were found that had been posted in the previous seven days.

Of the 67 job descriptions, 32 were for professional individual contributor positions and 35 were for managerial positions. The most common job titles were

▶ organization development and training specialist (individual contributor)
▶ organization development consultant (individual contributor)

▶ organization development specialist (individual contributor)
▶ senior OD consultant (individual contributor)
▶ organization development manager (managerial)
▶ director of organization effectiveness (managerial)
▶ director of OD (managerial)
▶ director, employee, and OD (managerial)
▶ senior director, OD, and training (managerial).

Other, less common, job titles included change management analyst, change management senior consultant, learning and OD consultant, OD analyst, OD and learning facilitator, organization effectiveness and engagement business professional, organization effectiveness specialist, organization change specialist, quality change management specialist, senior OD specialist, senior OD and learning specialist, strategic change consultant, training and OD consultant, change facilitator, director of change management, director of OD and talent management, director of organization and leadership development, executive director of talent management and OD, OD and training manager, organization effectiveness manager, and senior director/vice president of human resources and OD.

Noted

For individual contributor positions, 100 percent of the job descriptions listed facilitation as a major responsibility. For managerial positions, change management and organization alignment were listed most often (in 97 percent of managerial job descriptions).

Little consistency existed between job titles and job duties. There were significant differences in how each company interpreted the various roles and job responsibilities within the OD discipline. Job descriptions with "change management" in the title were the exception and tended to describe jobs focused on change management initiatives. Of the 67 job descriptions, only three fell into this narrow category.

Most of these advertised jobs were a combination of OD, training, and human resources roles. Seventy-six percent of the jobs were a hybrid of OD and training responsibilities, and 21 percent of the jobs were a hybrid of OD and human resources. In addition, 13 percent of the jobs were a hybrid of OD, training, and human resources roles. Only 16 percent of the jobs were narrowly focused on traditional OD work. Jobs with obvious hybrid titles, like OD and training manager, were outnumbered by seemingly OD-focused titles, like OD manager (which were often hybrid jobs despite the title). The title did not determine which jobs were pure OD and which were hybrids, making matters confusing for potential applicants.

Basic Rule 4
Organization development practitioners often hold jobs that combine OD, training, and human resources responsibilities.

Education is very important to employers hiring OD professionals. Employers preferred or required a master's degree in 37 percent of the individual contributor jobs and 75 percent of the managerial jobs. Only 3 percent of the jobs did not require a bachelor's degree or higher.

Noted

Many employers prefer applicants with a master's degree because they believe that OD practitioners need a strong behavioral sciences background to excel.

The job duties varied widely among the 67 job descriptions and within job descriptions with the same title. No accurate generalizations could be made about what is required of OD managers because the job descriptions were significantly different. Across the 67 job descriptions, these job responsibilities were listed most often:

- ▶ facilitating (mentioned in 96 percent of the job descriptions)
- ▶ consulting (mentioned in 94 percent of the job descriptions)
- ▶ coaching (mentioned in 94 percent of the job descriptions)
- ▶ aligning and designing the organization (mentioned in 88 percent of the job descriptions)
- ▶ managing change (mentioned in 85 percent of the job descriptions)

- ▶ improving performance (mentioned in 84 percent of the job descriptions)
- ▶ analyzing (mentioned in 82 percent of the job descriptions)
- ▶ shaping culture (mentioned in 79 percent of the job descriptions)
- ▶ learning strategy (mentioned in 79 percent of the job descriptions)
- ▶ leading and managing development (mentioned in 75 percent of the job descriptions)
- ▶ building the team (mentioned in 73 percent of the job descriptions)
- ▶ planning strategically (mentioned in 73 percent of the job descriptions).

These figures include the number of times these job responsibilities were listed on all the job descriptions. Table 2-1 shows how often roles included these responsibilities for individual contributor and managerial positions.

There were no significant differences between individual contributor and managerial job descriptions regarding which responsibilities or tasks topped the list. The expected level of expertise within these tasks was higher for managerial jobs.

Conclusions drawn from the analysis of these 67 job descriptions include

- ▶ Professionals interested in OD work at the managerial level should pursue their master's degree.

Table 2-1. Assessment for core organization development skills.

Job Responsibility	Individual Contributor Roles (% of 32 Job Descriptions)	Manager Roles (% of 35 Job Descriptions)
Facilitating	100%	91%
Consulting	94%	94%
Coaching	94%	94%
Aligning and Designing the Organization	78%	97%
Managing Change	72%	97%
Improving Performance	75%	91%
Analyzing	75%	89%
Shaping Culture	69%	89%
Learning Strategy	75%	83%
Leading and Managing Development	69%	80%
Building the Team	75%	71%
Planning Strategically	63%	83%

Think About This

If you are looking for a job in the OD field, you need to look beyond the job title. Search for OD, training, and human resources jobs, and read the job descriptions fully. In addition, provide examples of work that you have done that relate to the job requirements. If you do not have a master's degree, share your knowledge of the field and behavioral sciences models and methods.

▶ Most OD positions are a hybrid of training and OD responsibilities.

▶ Facilitating, consulting, and coaching services are most sought by employers.

▶ The field of OD is broad and interconnects with training and human resources. Successful OD practitioners can offer a wide variety of services that enable organizations to excel.

Core Skills

Organization development practitioners need a broad set of skills to provide employers with the value and results they seek. Some of these skills are obvious, while others may not be apparent based on the job description.

Here is a list of skills needed by OD practitioners. It does not include management and leadership skills needed to be successful in managerial positions, nor does it address the training or human resources skills required of hybrid positions. Organization development practitioners need to have the ability to effectively:

▶ Facilitate myriad business conversations for both small and large groups. (See chapters 6 and 7.)

▶ Consult with management and employees about organizational issues. This includes the ability to contract with clients to clarify and create agreement about initiative goals, expectations, and processes. (See chapter 6.)

▶ Coach managers, executives, and teams. (See chapters 8 and 9.)

▶ Build and maintain positive and trusting relationships with people at all levels of the organization and with diverse points of view. (See chapter 6.)

▶ Recognize and proactively deal with conflict and resistance. (See chapter 6.)

▶ Apply fundamental theories at the heart of OD work, including theories that address systems, change management, learning, group process, and performance. (See chapters 1, 3, 4, and 10.)

▶ Communicate theoretical and conceptual information to clients and stakeholders. (See chapters 3, 4, and 6.)

▶ Gather accurate and thorough information. (See chapters 3 and 4.)

▶ Analyze and redesign organization processes and structures. (See chapters 3 and 4.)

▶ Create, communicate, and implement organization alignment initiatives. (See chapters 3 and 4.)

▶ Design, communicate, and implement change initiatives. (See chapters 3, 4, and 5.)

▶ Link OD initiatives to broader corporate goals and measure initiative progress and success. (See chapter 6.)

▶ Assess and proactively intervene to reduce organization issues and barriers. (See chapter 6.)

▶ Embrace mistakes and surprises. (See chapters 6 and 7.)

▶ Apply systems thinking to organizational problems and opportunities. (See chapters 1, 3, and 4.)

▶ Navigate through ambiguity and apply solutions that improve goal and role clarity. (See chapter 6.)

▶ Become known as a valuable organization resource and sought by clients. (See chapters 6 and 8.) This is the hardest-to-define requirement, but may be the most important. Organization development practitioners can only be

Think About This

It is clear that companies define OD, training, and human resources roles differently. If you are interested in applying for an OD position, check out the company's human resources and training job descriptions, too. This will give you a better idea of what the company expects from OD practitioners and how the various roles interrelate or overlap. When interviewing, ask the hiring manager or recruiting professional how the roles are structured.

successful when their clients want to work with them. Are you easy to deal with? Do you help your clients get results? Do you offer practical and provocative coaching?

Basic Rule 5

Organization development practitioners need a wide range of skills to be successful. The most sought skills are facilitating, consulting, coaching, analyzing the organization, and managing change.

Does this list look daunting? At the beginning of their careers, OD practitioners do not need to possess each one of these skills to be successful. As your career grows, however, you will want to develop the capability to perform a broad set of OD tasks and initiatives.

Getting It Done

In this chapter, you were introduced to the many jobs held by OD practitioners and the skills most sought by employers. Trainers, managers, and human resources professionals have skills transferable to OD work. Exercise 2-1 will aid you in evaluating your current OD skills and experiences.

Exercise 2-1. Assessing your organization development skills and experiences.

For each of the skills listed, assess whether this is an area of strength or a potential development opportunity. For an additional point of view, ask your manager or a peer with which you closely work to fill out the worksheet.

Organization Development Skill	Strength	Potential Development
Facilitating		
Consulting		
Coaching		
Building and Maintaining Productive Partnerships		
Communicating with Clients		
Analyzing		
Aligning the Organization		
Managing Change and Interventions		
Systems Thinking		
Being a Catalyst		
Questioning/Interviewing		
Behavioral Sciences Knowledge		

In the next chapter, you will learn the most widely used model in organization development, action research.

3

The Action Research Approach to Change

■ ■

 What's Inside This Chapter

In this chapter, you'll learn:

▶ What *action research* means
▶ The phases of the action research model
▶ How to use the action research model to facilitate change
▶ A process for organization alignment.

The Action Research Model

Action research is the model that is most commonly used in OD initiatives. Chances are that you have already been using it, even if you did not know its name. The term *action research* first came from John Collier who, as the commissioner of Indian Affairs, experimented with several methods for bringing about positive changes in ethnic relations. Picking up on Collier's work, researcher Kurt Lewin conducted action research projects, which included many of the models and methods in use today.

Action research is both a model and a process. In its simplest form, action research is a process whereby research, or fact-finding, precedes action and follows it. The thought process looks something like this: Fact-finding—action—fact-finding—action—fact-finding—action, and so on. The action research process takes shape as understanding increases. The process remains focused on the desired state and how each systemic element needs to change. This approach to change and education can be found in many OD practices and methods.

Noted

Action research works much the same way as a guided missile stays on track. Guided missiles measure their progress and distance often and make small adjustments to ensure they hit their target. Action research is a process that begins with a desired state and makes adjustments as needed based on frequent measurements.

As a model, there are several phases that guide the OD practitioner and the client through change intervention with the goal of producing a desired state. The model uses the dynamic and iterative nature of action research in conjunction with fundamental consulting practices. The client and the OD practitioner continuously examine, reflect, and incorporate discoveries throughout the action research intervention.

Basic Rule 6

Action research is the model underlying many organization development activities.

There are several versions of the action research model, but they have common themes. Figure 3-1 shows a simplified model that includes the elements found in most action research approaches.

Entry

Action research begins with a client who has a need or desire. At this phase, the OD practitioner and the client have preliminary conversations about the desired state and a potential change initiative. This phase may last minutes or may be an evolving conversation over one or more weeks. The OD practitioner's goals during entry should be to determine who wants the change, gauge commitment for the change, understand the

Figure 3-1. Action research model.

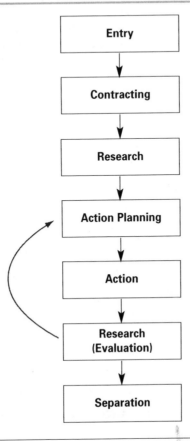

change that is sought (in broad terms), develop a relationship with the client, and get a feel for the general issues involved in the initiative. If the OD practitioner is unknown to the client, the OD practitioner will want to share related experiences.

Noted

There is a difference between commitment to a desired state and commitment for the change process. The OD practitioner should offer information and ask questions that help the client understand the breadth of the changes needed to reach the desired state. Many change interventions fail due to a lack of commitment and resources needed to fully implement a change process.

Contracting

The goals of the intervention are defined, and the client and the OD practitioner agree on the roles that the client, the OD practitioner, and the stakeholders will play. Change efforts are more successful when both the client and the stakeholders participate in the process. The OD practitioner often takes on the primary role of facilitator and coach. In addition, the OD practitioner is expected to be an expert in matters relating to how organizations, cultures, and people change.

Think About This

Contracting can be a formal or relatively informal process. For large interventions, the OD practitioner will want to get agreements written down and described in detail. For many projects, however, the contracting can be done in a friendly, verbal conversation that establishes how you and your client want to work together.

During contracting, the OD practitioner and the client should also agree on how data will be collected; how and when the data feedback will occur; and the project's goals, plan, scope, participants, measures, and timeline. The OD practitioner works with the client to define desired outcomes and assess the client's willingness to embark on the intervention. What if a significant shift in current practices is required, how far is the client willing to go to get to the desired state? The OD practitioner establishes the current theories for why the change is needed and how the problems/challenges have occurred.

Contracting will take several hours of meeting time. At this stage, the client and the OD practitioner agree on the overall boundaries of the project, including any areas or topics that are off limits. The client and the OD practitioner agree on ground rules for the working relationship, including agreements about confidentiality, meeting frequency, and communication protocol. Table 3-1 offers a set of questions that you can use as a contracting checklist.

Research

(Note: Some action research models separate research into two phases: data collection and feedback.) Organization development practitioners take a systematic approach to

Table 3-1. Contracting worksheet.

Contracting Questions	Agreement
What are the goals of the intervention? What are the milestones and timeline for the intervention?	
What roles will the OD practitioner and the client play?	
Who will be involved in the intervention? Should the OD practitioner contact individuals directly, or does the client want to let them know the OD practitioner will be contacting them?	
Who are the key stakeholders, and what type of communications will the OD practitioner have with them?	
What needs to be measured, and are there restrictions or preferences for how the data is collected? Are there limitations on who can participate?	
What ground rules should the OD practitioner and the client use?	
How will the OD practitioner and the client communicate, and how frequently should the OD practitioner update the client on the project's progress?	
Are there specials concerns or considerations the OD practitioner should be aware of?	
What is the overall priority of this work relative to other projects?	

fact-finding. They assess how roles, processes, practices, systems, culture, the external environment, skills, technology, goals, and communication will need to change to reach the desired outcomes. The OD practitioner often begins with interviews, data analyses, and workflow diagrams, but other research techniques include surveys, observations, and brainstormings. Involving stakeholders in the fact-finding phase is critical for two reasons. First, the stakeholders are often the most knowledgeable; and second, involving them early improves buy-in for later changes. As data collection is under way, the OD practitioner develops theories about how to best enable the organization to reach

Think About This

During the contracting phase, the client and the OD practitioner agree to the scope and nature of interviews. Even so, the OD practitioner should be sensitive to political and cultural considerations regarding who should be interviewed and how. For example, many senior leaders prefer one-on-one discussions over group interviews. Group interviews can be effective for some topics, but are less successful in situations where the group is tense or dialogue is affected by looming, undiscussible topics. In these situations, individual interviews will yield better information. Although not always practical or possible, it is recommended that you conduct individual interviews.

Noted

It is important that the OD practitioner maintain a calm and objective demeanor throughout the change process. Displaying emotions, like anger, disappointment, or shock, can have a negative effect on the level of trust and collaboration between the OD practitioner and the client or stakeholders. Read more about important behavioral considerations in chapter 6.

its desired state. These theories should fuel additional fact-finding and conversations to determine whether each theory is on target.

Once the initial research is complete, the OD practitioner reviews the data with the client. Depending upon what was agreed to during the contracting phase, the OD practitioner will either share his or her theories or the client and the OD practitioner will discuss the theories together. In either case, the focus is on using the information to determine the key organizational levers that should be adjusted to help the organization get to its desired state.

It is often helpful to present the data in a graphic format that will facilitate understanding and dialogue. The data should hit on all aspects of the system, including the structure, roles, systems, processes, culture, rewards and reinforcements, skills, management and leadership (a subset of structure, but important to call out), technology, and communication. Assessment and feedback often lead into the action planning phase, but do not rush it. It is important that the client has the time to understand, think about, and accept the data. Based on the feedback session(s) and the questions that have risen, the OD practitioner and the client may choose to collect additional information or move on to the action planning phase.

Think About This

It is a good idea to share the data with senior management or the client before meeting with a broader group. If the data is being shared with a group of people, it is courteous to share the information with the client first, a day or two before the feedback meeting. The client does not want to be surprised, and he or she might be able to offer additional information or context for the data that will be beneficial to share at the feedback meeting. Sharing the data does not mean that the client can change it, so the OD practitioner will need to be clear about that. Sharing the information with the client before others is a professional courtesy and enables the client to prepare his or her response or reaction.

Action Planning

The OD practitioner and the client have reviewed the data and are now ready to craft an initial plan. Often the OD practitioner is asked to create a draft plan for review with the client. Sometimes the client prefers to create the initial plan with the OD practitioner. In inclusive environments, a team of people craft the plan together. (This is ideal.) The initial plan should answer these questions:

- ▶ What is the picture/vision?
- ▶ What will change (roles, processes, structure, practices, projects)?
- ▶ Who is involved?
- ▶ How will changes be communicated?
- ▶ When will changes occur?
- ▶ How will the OD practitioner and the client help people transition? (See chapter 5.)
- ▶ How will changes be monitored and measured?
- ▶ What does success look like?
- ▶ What resources are required?
- ▶ What OD methods will be used to effect the changes?

The action planning phase is critical, and you should allow enough time to develop a thorough plan. This is particularly important when designing role and structure changes. Be sure to define how roles will change and how these changes will affect other roles, processes, and projects.

The OD practitioner recommends methods to facilitate various changes. For example, should there be a large-group intervention to kick off the process? Will small-group training sessions be required? Do processes need to undergo a realignment effort? Should leaders receive coaching? Will the changes warrant modifications to the performance-management systems? Should the intervention include a process for culture change? Does change need to begin with strategic planning or visioning? More information about the application of these and other OD methods is included in subsequent chapters. Factors that affect which methods should be employed during the intervention include

- the scope of the change—the amount of the system that will be affected
- the areas of greatest need—skills, technology, processes
- the number of people involved in the change
- the level of resistance to the change
- the organization's current culture and readiness for the change.

Think About This

Which OD methods should you use as part of a change intervention? The experience of the OD practitioner will be most apparent during the action planning phase. There are many ways to create a particular outcome, and it is important to consider methods and practices that are the best match for the organization and the client. Early in their careers, OD practitioners should consult with other OD practitioners to generate several options to consider. It might be necessary to hire outside OD professionals to execute particular projects or events.

Most change initiatives underestimate the need for and value of communication. Organization development practitioners should help the client structure regular and open communication sessions that inform employees about changes and serve as a forum to discuss questions and concerns. This should be a condition of moving forward with the initiative. The result of the action planning stage is an intervention plan.

Action

This is the phase of action research that is the "action." Together, the OD practitioner, the client, and the stakeholders launch the intervention. It is important to monitor each action thoroughly and make immediate adjustments if warranted. The OD practitioner should regularly update the client and err on the side of over-communication. A well-planned action phase will include a few early wins to give the intervention attention and positive momentum. The intervention plan should focus on desired outcomes and intermediary milestones.

Noted

Bridges

Kick-off events help mark the ending of what's changing and articulate the new beginning. The kick-off does not have to be large or lavish, but there should be some meeting or event that marks the beginning of the change process and prepares employees for what is coming.

Various elements of the intervention can occur concurrently, but beware of causing confusion or bumping against limitations of capacity. Clients can be eager to implement changes and may initially overcommit people or other resources. (This is quite common.) If this occurs, quickly adjust the plan. It is more important to execute the intervention well than to get it done quickly.

Research (Evaluation)

Action research works because action follows research and research follows action, as pictured in figure 3-2. It is a process of staying in action while evaluating along the way. This is an important part of the model because it is difficult to predict how various elements of an intervention will work and interrelate. Sometimes results are better than expected, sometimes results are disappointing, and sometimes results are just different than planned. The OD practitioner should facilitate a review of the data gathered since launching the intervention and encourage lively dialogue with the client about the results. New learning has been occurring, and you want to take advantage of this knowledge. Data should be presented in a form that is most helpful and was negotiated during the contracting phase. Often, the OD practitioner will present information colored with anecdotal reports from key stakeholders. It is best to offer both quantitative and qualitative data.

Figure 3-2. Interactive nature of action research.

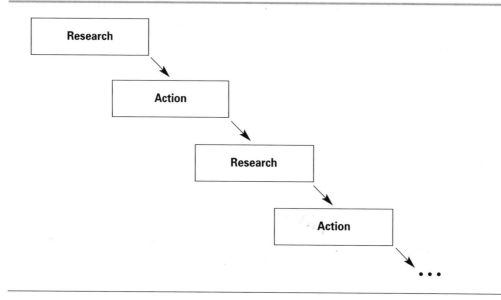

Basic Rule 7

The iterative process of research, then action, then research is fundamental to the action research approach and many OD methods.

The OD practitioner should resist the need to vigorously defend actions that are not working or are being questioned. The objective is to implement actions that will work and be supported. It is not helpful to become personally invested in any particular method or action. Another goal of action planning is to help the organization build its capacity to learn, plan, and manage change. The OD practitioner should strive to leave each intervention having helped the organization become stronger and more able.

If there is still important work to be done before reaching the desired state, the process continues at the action planning phase. If the results are satisfactory and the client feels ready to complete the intervention, the change process moves into the separation phase. This phase includes planning for maintaining the progress that has already been achieved.

Separation

The separation phase serves two purposes. First, the OD practitioner will share recommendations for how to maintain the progress achieved by the intervention. These recommendations should be detailed and highly actionable. The easier it is to support the changes, the better. The OD practitioner should also offer summarized documentation of the change effort.

Noted

A good separation is something to celebrate! Some OD practitioners resist separation or never fully separate. Separation means this intervention is complete. It does not mean that the work with this client is done.

The second purpose of the separation phase is to end the consultant-client relationship (relative to this intervention) on a high note. There comes a time in the project where it is clear that time is better spent on other projects. The OD practitioner should plan a final meeting with the client to request feedback about the relationship and the process (the communication, methods, facilitation, results, variety and quality of recommendations, effectiveness of the coaching, and development of the plan).

While the phases of action research have been presented in a neat and sequential manner, it does not always go this way. The OD practitioner should use the action research model flexibly to meet the client's needs and fit within the organization's culture. For example, in more dynamic environments, action planning and action may occur concurrently. Research and action planning may need to occur at the same time. When working on a very large change effort, it may be wise to pilot the change effort with a small group before launching the process across the organization. It is also common for the pace and commitment level to change midway through the project.

Organization Alignment—Ensuring the Organization Is Set Up for Success

A well-aligned organization hums with efficiency. Processes flow well and are effective. Employee roles are clear and focused on the most important work. Individuals are appropriately empowered and held accountable for producing results. Communication among departments is collaborative and enables each team to head off problems and prioritize. The organizational structure facilitates great dialogue and problem solving. Work is satisfying because it makes sense.

Few organizations are ever fully aligned because changes are occurring at breakneck speed. Poorly aligned organizational structures and processes cause numerous problems with quality, throughput, and results. When a structure or process is out of alignment, it no longer serves the goals of the team or company. Poor alignment can occur for various reasons, such as a change occurring in one area, but not in others. Sometimes the trouble is a lack of effective processes for getting the work done. Or it could be that roles have changed but processes have not, or vice versa.

A common reason for poor alignment is conflict among technology, processes, and roles. For team members, a poorly aligned organization feels disorganized, and getting work done seems more difficult. Ambiguous, confusing, and overlapping roles are also signs of poor alignment. Many clients assume that unproductive people are to blame for poor results. While there may be personnel problems for the client to resolve, it is more likely that the department's processes and structures are responsible for poor results.

The organization structure defines job roles, departmental interdependencies, and communication channels. Structure determines who makes the decisions and the depth and breadth of each person's role. Structure assigns responsibilities and accountabilities. The structure is part of the overall organization system that includes processes, practices, and culture.

The following sections describe practices that help OD practitioners ensure that systemic-organization elements are relevant and aligned. These practices begin by asking one fundamental question: *Is this organization set up for success?* Organization development practitioners should regularly ask this question because keeping roles and processes aligned is critical to ensuring optimal throughput and results. Start by looking at the big picture, then focus on aspects of the system that need attention to deliver results.

Basic Rule 8

Organization realignment is a process that helps ensure various elements of an organization's system are set up to support the company's goals.

Noted

Processes are ways of working within a structure. They may be as elaborate as a computer-controlled manufacturing line or as simple as a way to deliver interoffice mail. There are also de facto processes, or processes that have evolved and become standard practice without intentional design or planning. These processes need to be acknowledged and included in the organization alignment.

As is the case for most interventions, the process starts with contracting with the client. Figure 3-3 shows the typical steps you will take to realign the organization.

Organization development practitioners may also be asked to help an organization recover from a poorly implemented change. In this case, you will want to refer to the previous sections on action research and chapter 5.

Clarify the Vision, Purpose, and Goals

It is important that each department's vision and purpose are inspiring and represent its contribution to the business. Here is an example of what the vision, purpose, and goals might look like for an accounting group:

▶ *Vision:* There is an expectation that, as the functional experts, the team will oversee the organization as it follows appropriate procedures to ensure fiscal accuracy and compliance with regulations and audit principles. As the organization increases its presence on the Internet, it expects the accounting team to support and process sales transactions that come over the Website.

▶ *Purpose:* The accounting group is an internal service team and has an opportunity and responsibility to provide timely and beneficial services, information, practical analysis, effective solutions, and thorough answers to inquiries to both internal and external customers.

▶ *Goals:* Over the next year, the accounting team's four major goals are to

1. Improve the efficiency of invoice processing by reducing errors by 50 percent, and improve processing speed by 15 percent while maintaining or improving current processing costs.

Figure 3-3. Organization alignment.

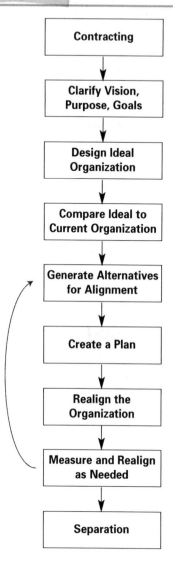

2. Improve purchasing and billing processes related to field operations, including improving purchase order and invoice transmittal and reducing the cost of the processing by 10 percent or more.

3. Design and launch accurate and helpful reports that enable department supervisors to manage their areas more proactively and effectively. This

effort should lead to an overall reduction in budget variances by the third month of implementation. Eliminate obsolete reports.

4. Create and implement a strategy that supports the company's plans for selling products and services on its Website. Develop online shopping cart services and reconciliation methods to ensure the proper collection and management of revenues.

Noted

A department's vision describes the desired future state. The purpose describes the ideal contribution the group makes to the company. The goals are the most important changes, improvements, or projects that the group will embark upon over the next year to realize its purpose and move toward the vision.

Think About This

Departments often see their vision and purpose much smaller than is optimal. Many people have not thought about their functions in these terms before. You may need to help teams think big by providing inspiring examples and asking questions that help them examine their purpose and vision fully. To create a meaningful purpose, ask questions about why the function is critical to the company's success.

Design an Ideal Organization Model, Process, and Culture

This phase of the realignment is important and should not be shortchanged. Consider charting the discussion as it develops so that the team can visualize the design. If you do not use the appreciative inquiry model (discussed in chapter 4), these questions will get you started:

▶ What is the long-term direction of the company, and how should the manager and the team design today's work with this in mind?

▶ What is the most important work this team could do?

▶ What needs to be accomplished to meet or exceed the team's goals? Look at each goal individually, then as a whole.

▶ To do this work, what roles are required? How should the department divide work among individuals and teams?

▶ How should managers and team members make decisions?

▶ What should the key processes be and how should they work? What processes would make the work easier and more efficient?

▶ What role should technology play?

▶ How would the team and process link to the rest of the company?

▶ What are the advantages and disadvantages of this organization design?

▶ What human, process, and technology resources are needed to make this organization structure work?

▶ If there were no limitations on resources, how would you and your team design the department's structure?

If possible, involve the entire team in creating this design. In addition to clarifying the roles, it is important to identify the processes that would make the work easier and more efficient. Depending on the scope and breadth of the work you are assessing, this could take several hours to a few days.

Compare the Ideal to Current Systemic Elements

Once the ideal organizational design is complete, OD practitioners should bring the current reality into the realignment process and conversation. It is important to include a discussion of de facto processes. There are generally many more processes in place than managers recognize. For example, communication and problem resolution are areas where de facto processes are common.

Think About This

When helping a group create the ideal organization, it is important to help them set aside the constraints of the current reality and think from a blue-sky perspective. Continuously challenge their ideas and ask whether this model represents the ideal organization. Bring in current business magazines or industry trade journals to generate inspiring ideas. Don't call the process complete until you are sure that they have created the ideal organization.

For each area of the ideal organization, note the current conditions and highlight key barriers, gaps, and restrictions (like regulatory requirements). You should also indicate where there are gaps but no major barriers getting in the way of moving to the ideal state. It is important to thoroughly explore cultural elements as they may be some of the more important and difficult elements to change. For example, the ideal state may call for a nimble, transition-enabled, and innovative culture. The current state may be quite the opposite. It is important to emphasize the changes in assumptions, beliefs, practices, leadership, and policies that would need to be addressed to create the cultural change.

Generate Alternatives That Improve the Organization's Alignment

During this part of the realignment, the team will need to blend the ideal scenario with current roles, personnel, and processes. There are always going to be some compromises required. It is important to stand firm for the changes that are most important and be flexible and nimble in areas where multiple approaches might work.

The team should ask and explore these questions to fully understand what they are about to begin:

- ▶ How far apart is the ideal organization model from the current state? What are the differences and similarities?
- ▶ Is the ideal organization possible and practical?
- ▶ If the ideal organization is worth attaining (it should be if you asked the right questions), what might a transitional organization look like? How can the department begin its journey to ideal alignment?
- ▶ What aspects and processes of the current organization should not be changed? Why?

Think About This

Groups will tend to be conservative when comparing the ideal state to the current reality. You want the group to consider all barriers and gaps, but you should question them on whether these challenges can be overcome. Make sure that they are not jumping to conclusions about what can and cannot change.

▶ What further information or research do you and your team need to understand these ideas and choices? (Do this analysis and research before making decisions.)

▶ What objections or concerns will senior management or peers have about these ideas? Are they valid? How can you and your team overcome these objections?

Notice where the team is struggling or where its thinking might need to be challenged. After this phase, you will know the ideas on the table and the pros and cons of each. You will also have a good idea of how much needs to change to create alignment. This is a useful and illuminating process.

A word about team-member participation: The general rule is that you should include input from team members and peers as much as possible. Depending on the nature of the realignment, it may not be appropriate to include team members in discussions about redesigning roles and processes. If jobs might be eliminated, then team members should not participate in the final design of roles. If team members ask whether jobs might be cut (they are probably wondering even if they do not ask), it is best that the manager be open and honest. The purpose of the organizational realignment and redesign is to figure out how the department can be more efficient and effective. This may mean that some processes and jobs will change, but the final details will not be clear until the realignment plan is complete and approved. If people are likely to be affected, you should help your client get through the redesign process as quickly as possible. If the organizational realignment is going to be significant and include major role changes, it might be best to complete the entire

Think About This

Use visuals throughout this realignment process. It is helpful to commandeer a war room and plaster the walls with the ideal state, the current state, the gaps, and the alignment alternatives. If a war room is not available, use charts that can be taken down and put up every time the group meets. It is helpful if the team continually refers to the ideal state when designing realignment alternatives. You may also want to use a computer program that offers technology-driven solutions, like mind mapping and business-process mapping programs.

redesign process confidentially and without team-member participation. That said, if team members are not included in the redesign process, you will need to take other steps to ensure the design team has thorough and accurate information from which to make decisions.

Create a Plan for Realigning Systemic Elements

This is the phase of the realignment where senior management is briefed (if they have not been involved throughout the process). The team should create two or three realignment approaches based on the information collected and discussions that have occurred. If there is one alternative that is significantly better than the other possible plans, then present only one plan. Because more than one workable scenario often exists, it is best to prepare and present more than one option. As the planning progresses, the team may eliminate choices based on criteria, including cost, ease of use, technology, or a hassle factor. The exception to this rule is when the team feels confident and positive about an organizational design it has created. If it has done its homework and included the appropriate people in discussions, then it should present this recommendation and sell it with passion to the key stakeholders and decision makers. Energy and passion account for much of the success of any plan. Whether presenting one or more alternatives, each plan should include

▶ a review of the vision, purpose, and goals the realignment seeks to support
▶ a review of the proposed realigned organization and processes, and the results that the proposed organization will produce
▶ a plan for transition of personnel roles and processes
▶ a description of roles and interdependencies between team members
▶ a description of major processes
▶ an explanation of how the work will flow among groups
▶ a breakdown of short-term and long-term costs.

Depending on the scope of the plan, preparing it could take anywhere from a few hours to a couple of weeks. Don't rush the process if more analysis and creativity will make the plan significantly better. As the plan is coming together, encourage a manager to play devil's advocate and challenge the plan to ensure that it answers potential objections and meets the needs of supporters and naysayers. It is useful to present the plan to a small group and ask for their input (provided the information is appropriate to share). Help the team adjust the plan based on this feedback.

Think About This

Help the team dry run the plan several times and get as much input as practical. Even when you have included a wide variety of people throughout the planning stages, it is inevitable that one or more perspectives are left out and not addressed. The dry runs will help surface any additional perspectives, and you can have the group consider the input as needed before the final presentation.

The team presents the plan and gains approval! They should provide backup information and details as needed. The OD practitioner should ensure that the team takes the time to prepare for the presentation of the plan, as this will speed up its approval.

Realign the Organization

The implementation of new structures and processes is critical to the success of the realignment. To ensure that team members and peers support the new way of doing the work, the OD practitioner should

- ▶ Work with management and human resources on the timing of the plan's implementation, especially if any individual jobs or positions are affected.
- ▶ Coach the client, the managers, and the team members on ways to communicate the vision, the realignment plan, the transition plan, and the role of each team member. They also need to share the plan with peers and gain their support. Timing of communications is critical. If an individual's job is changing significantly, the managers should talk to him or her one-on-one before any team announcements occur.

The communication plan should include

- ▶ a rollout or general announcement (see chapter 5)
- ▶ a clear plan for the transition of roles and processes
- ▶ daily or weekly progress chats as needed.

The client, the managers, the team members, and the OD practitioner should be available and ready to listen to any concerns, suggestions, or questions.

Be flexible enough to accept that the plan may need to be altered. Take time every day to check in with the client and the design team. Do not micromanage the process, but show support and invite feedback.

Measure the Progress, and Realign as Needed

As the realignment rolls out and takes hold, it is important to monitor and measure performance and productivity. After all, that is why changes were made in the first place. Measures should be communicated clearly and discussed often. Key measures and milestones should be posted in a visible place in the department.

In an aligned organization, hassles go down and the work environment is more intrinsically motivating. It runs like a well-oiled machine. To ensure the organization stays aligned, it needs to be evaluated regularly and as changes occur. While there are always elements of the system that need realignment, it is a good idea to evaluate the overall alignment of departments every two years, and then follow up with smaller redesign efforts as needed. For example, if your company launches a new product line, a portion of the department's work, processes, and roles may need realignment.

Getting It Done

In this chapter, you learned about the action research model for change implementation and an approach to organization alignment. The action research model may seem a bit daunting until you try it. Use exercise 3-1 to generate ideas for applying action research.

Exercise 3-1. Ideas for applying action research.

Use this exercise to generate ideas for ways you can apply action research in your organization.

Organizational Changes That Might Call for Action Research	Your Organization
List the changes that your company is struggling with.	
Given the company's goals and vision for the future, what changes are imminent?	
List any major product-development projects.	
List any systems upgrade projects occurring in the next year.	
List cultural changes that would help the company become more competitive and successful.	

Use exercise 3-2 to assess the alignment of the organization relative to one of its major goals.

Exercise 3-2. Assessing organization alignment.

List one of your company's major goals for the year.

_____

Indicate whether the following systemic elements are aligned for optimal success and the reason why you believe this. Share your thoughts with your manager or client.

Systemic Elements	Aligned for Success	Why
Structure	☐ Yes ☐ No	
Culture	☐ Yes ☐ No	
Processes	☐ Yes ☐ No	
Practices	☐ Yes ☐ No	
Goals	☐ Yes ☐ No	
Organization metrics	☐ Yes ☐ No	

Systemic Elements	Aligned for Success	Why
Communication and decision-making processes	☐ Yes ☐ No	
Technology	☐ Yes ☐ No	
Workflow	☐ Yes ☐ No	
Skills	☐ Yes ☐ No	
Management practices	☐ Yes ☐ No	

In the next chapter, you will learn about a popular and relatively new model for organization changes called *appreciative inquiry.*

4

The Appreciative Inquiry
Approach to Change

▪▪

What's Inside This Chapter

In this chapter, you'll learn:

▶ The definition of appreciative inquiry
▶ Fundamental assumptions about organization change and learning
▶ Phases of the 4-D cycle
▶ The approach to appreciative inquiry.

Appreciative inquiry is an affirmative approach to personal and organization transformation. The appreciative inquiry approach is based on the assumption that positive questions and conversations about visions, values, successes, and strengths have the power to enliven possibilities and engage people in creating exciting, new realities. David Cooperrider, Suresh Srivastva, and their colleagues at Case Western Reserve University developed appreciative inquiry in the 1980s. According to Cooperrider in *The Power of Appreciative Inquiry* (Whitney and Trosten-Bloom),

The aim of appreciative inquiry is to help the organization in:

1. Envisioning a collectively desired future, and
2. Carrying forth that vision in ways that successfully translate intention into reality, and beliefs into practices (2003).

At the core of appreciative inquiry is a belief that reality is socially constructed—that the world is created in conversation. When conversations focus on strengths, possibilities, and vision, the reality is more likely positive and inspirational. When conversations focus on problems, complaints, and weaknesses, those things become more prominent and real. According to the appreciative inquiry approach, if the OD practitioner and the client take a problem-solving approach to change, this will limit their ability to create a new and exciting future. The appreciative inquiry approach focuses on opportunities and possibilities, not problems. By having open and positive conversations about success and what's possible, interventions produce more desirable results.

Noted

Social constructionism focuses on how interaction and social practices contribute to the way in which people define what is real or has meaning. Talk creates reality.

For the OD practitioner, appreciative inquiry is an approach that can be used in a variety of consulting and coaching situations, including change interventions and general facilitation. Appreciative inquiry creates a context for inclusion and participation and can transform traditional hierarchical organizations into workplaces characterized by collaboration, engagement, and partnership. Appreciative inquiry can help managers transition from an authoritarian to a more empowering style because it is participative and inclusive. It is also useful for helping renew and reengage professionals who have been stuck in a routine.

Noted

A common way to begin a change process is to look at what isn't working and start solving the problem. This process can become negative and will limit the options you consider. Appreciative inquiry questions are positive, hopeful, and focused on successes and what is possible. Appreciative inquiry questions leave people feeling confident, excited, and creative.

Appreciative inquiry is an approach that shifts the focus of analysis and dialogue from problems and concerns to opportunities and visions. Like action research, appreciative inquiry uses research, feedback, action planning, and action to implement robust change interventions. The difference is what's being looked at and talked about. Problems still exist and are acknowledged when using an appreciative inquiry approach, but they are framed to focus on what's possible in the future. For example, a problem of high turnover would become an inquiry into what being an employer of choice might look like. A problem of long product-development cycles would become an inquiry that explores product-development strengths and the creation of a vision for world-class product development. These may seem like subtle changes, but they are not. Shifting the focus and conversation to the affirmative opens up participation and creativity. Appreciative inquiry unleashes employees' passions and power.

So, is appreciative inquiry a touchy-feely approach? Not at all. It is a powerful tool that can improve business productivity and results. In fact, OD practitioners who use appreciative inquiry find that the approach can yield much quicker results than problem-solving–based approaches. Appreciative inquiry engages participants and produces more and better ideas and cuts down on resistance to change. The appreciative inquiry approach honors current strengths and builds upon them to help participants build a vision and plan for the future.

Basic Rule 9
An affirmative approach to change, like that of appreciative inquiry, generates more ideas about what's possible and reduces resistance to change.

Appreciative inquiry is an approach that requires inclusion. Your appreciative inquiry interventions will be more successful if all employees (and maybe even vendors or customers) participate in the process. In general, more and broader perspectives are better. Because the appreciative inquiry process is inclusive, it reduces resistance to changes that might occur later.

The 4-D Cycle
David Cooperrider and Suresh Srivastva developed the 4-D cycle to guide OD practitioners and clients through the appreciative inquiry approach. The 4-D cycle can

Think About This

If you want to introduce the appreciative inquiry approach to your client, be cognizant that the name *appreciative inquiry* might be an initial barrier. (Some people think the name sounds too people focused and not enough results focused.) To gain interest and commitment, concentrate on the approach's ability to improve results and address important organizational challenges. Say your company is struggling with meeting project deadlines. Using a traditional problem-solving approach, you would generate a healthy list of potential solutions to the problem of late projects. Using an appreciative inquiry approach, you could generate ideas and commitment for masterful project execution. This work would offer a wider variety of possibilities and engage participants such that they feel a high level of commitment to and interest in the change.

be used for large or small change interventions. Organization development practitioners can even use the 4-D cycle when coaching individuals and teams. The elements of the 4-D cycle are listed in figure 4-1.

Topic

The appreciative inquiry approach starts with identifying the topic that the team will discuss and reinvent. The OD practitioner and the client should carefully select the topic, as this will set the tone for the inquiry. The topic should be something important to the company and an area that, if improved, would make a big difference. To select the topic, answer the question, *What do we want more of?* Here are several sample topics:

- making this company the employer of choice
- speeding up the product-development process
- delighting customers
- streaming new revenue
- visioning ideas for growth
- producing quality products
- innovating service.

Figure 4-1. 4-D cycle.

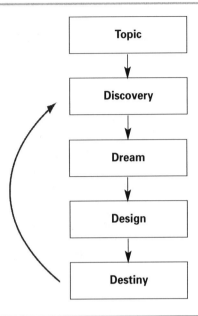

Good topics focus the conversation in a positive and powerful way and communicate what's important. Topics should clearly be desirable, stimulating, and related to the organization's future. Table 4-1 shows several examples of how you can reframe problems into excellent appreciative inquiry topics.

Discovery

The OD practitioner conducts appreciative interviews that uncover current best practices, strengths, and strategic capabilities. The appreciative interview is an important

Noted

"Appreciative Inquiry is the study and exploration of what gives life to human systems when they function at their best. This approach to personal change and organization change is based on the assumption that questions and dialogue about strengths, successes, values, hopes, and dreams are themselves transformational." (Whitney and Trosten-Bloom, The Power of Appreciative Inquiry *[2003])*

Table 4-1. Defining problems as opportunities.

Problem Statement	Opportunity
Turnover is too high.	How can we create a work environment that attracts and retains the best talent?
Projects are not getting done on time.	How can we master project success, implementation, execution, and results?
Our customer base is not growing fast enough to support new product introductions.	Who are our customers of today and tomorrow, and how can we find and build a relationship with them?
Our costs are out of line with revenues and need to be cut.	What is the model of optimal efficiency and alignment for our organization?
Our employees do not have the needed skills and are not performing up to expectations.	How can we create a learning organization where employees grow and help the organization respond to change needs?

part of the appreciative inquiry approach. The interview often starts with questions that ask participants to recall successes, high points, and times of full engagement related to the topic. The interviewer (often the OD practitioner) will also ask about learning experiences and visions, and how an optimal future would look.

To plan for the interviews, the OD practitioner will need to prepare an introduction of the topic and construct the interview questions. Creating great questions is important, so the OD practitioner should research appreciative inquiry questions and review sample interviews (see Additional Resources). Depending on the size of the appreciative inquiry intervention, the OD practitioner may need to train additional interviewers.

Appreciative interviews may be done one-on-one or in group meetings. The discovery phase of appreciative inquiry kick-starts positive conversations about the topic and generates constructive stories about the organization's strengths and successes. It prepares the organization for the rest of the appreciative inquiry process. Table 4-2 offers example appreciative inquiry interview questions. After looking at the samples, craft several questions of your own.

Dream

The dream phase of appreciative inquiry is a participative discovery of what's possible. Participants explore and discuss their visions, hopes, ideas, and dreams for the

Table 4-2. Creating appreciative inquiry questions.

Example Appreciative Inquiry Interview Questions	Your Questions
Tell me about how you came to work for "company X." What attracted you about the position and what were your hopes for what you would achieve?	
We all have special talents and strengths and contribute to the company's success. What are your special skills and talents?	
What is an experience that you enjoyed and would consider one of the high points since working for "company X"?	
What two or three changes would make "company X" the best it can be in terms of results and being a great place to work?	
Every company has special strengths and capabilities. What's special about "company X"?	

future. The OD practitioner, or other facilitator, will lead large-group discussions that help participants explore hopes and dreams for work, relationships, and organizational goals. Together, they think big and beyond where they have in the past. Boundaries are broken, and anything is possible.

Think About This

You might find it difficult to get a group of people to participate fully in an inquiry about what's possible. People's to-do lists are waiting, and you want them to take time to discuss what's never going to happen? You can help your clients embrace and focus on this process by ensuring them it will enhance the quality of the plan in the end. By the time the process is complete, you will have won them over, but it is sometimes difficult to get them engaged at the beginning of the process. Respect their time, and hold the meetings at convenient times and at an easily accessible location. Consider offering to pick up the tab for an extended two-hour working lunch.

The goal of the dream phase is to create a powerful and amazing vision for the future related to the topic. For example, the vision might be the best way to create and execute projects or to create a partnership with customers in new product development. The vision could also relate to the internal workings of the organization, like how to build cross-functional relationships and creative communities. To enable the best outcome, the OD practitioner or facilitator will want to employ methods that enliven creativity and participation. Table 4-3 lists example questions to address during the dream phase.

Table 4-3. Dream phase questions.

Example Appreciative Inquiry Dream Phase Questions
Project your thinking out five years (adjust number of years to fit the topic). "Company X" has been extremely successful in exceeding its vision and goals. What does this future look like?
How is the company viewed in the marketplace?
What is it like to work here in this future?
How is the organization structured? How is work done?
Describe the organization culture that is in place.

Design

The work done thus far is synthesized into a picture or model of what should change. Depending on the topic, this might mean creating a new organization plan, a set of operating practices, or a process map. Participants consider the organization's strengths and vision and determine how this should affect the structure, roles, processes, development, and practices. The design phase is a time to remain creative and optimistic while considering how to realign various parts of the organization to the new vision for the future.

The output of the design phase is a view of the desired state expressed in powerful statements called *provocative propositions*. Here is how David Cooperrider (2002) describes them:

> A provocative proposition is a statement that bridges the best of "what is" with your own speculation or intuition of "what might be." It is provocative to the extent to which it stretches the realm of the status quo, challenges common assumptions or routines, and helps suggest real possibilities that represent desired possibilities for the organization and its people.

Destiny

This phase correlates with both the action planning and the action phases of action research. Participants celebrate what they have created and set actions and projects in motion to make the vision a reality. Project teams may be assigned to make specific changes or to investigate options and approaches. Additional appreciative inquiry projects may also be spawned.

The destiny phase continues the positive momentum and allows highly motivated people to create the future they envisioned. The OD practitioner and the client must be mindful of the support structure that will be needed to ensure the work remains on the fore of people's minds and lists of priorities. Another goal of the destiny phase is to expand the use of the appreciative inquiry approach throughout the organization. There is a self-reinforcing nature of using positive and affirmative inquiry to improve the business.

The 4-D cycle starts with dreams and ends with substantive changes in the organization's practices, processes, systems, and structures. Like action research, appreciative inquiry is an approach that is self-correcting and iterative. Organization development practitioners who try appreciative inquiry need to be ready to see the process and outcomes take on a life of their own. The outcome cannot be determined up front. This is the case anytime you maximize inclusion, participation, and creativity. That the outcome cannot be predicted should not dissuade you from trying appreciative inquiry; the results are generally better and more interesting than you can imagine.

Think About This

To practice asking and answering appreciative inquiry questions, begin with your own goals. Write several questions and then answer them for yourself to create a powerful vision for your future. Try this with a friend or colleague as well. You will likely experience that it is motivating and energizing to think big and remain open to new possibilities. Notice how the conversation makes your friend feel. Follow through by creating plans for yourself and your friend that bridge the gap of today's reality and plot a path for reaching your visions for the future.

Using Appreciative Inquiry

Organization development practitioners unfamiliar with appreciative inquiry should not attempt a large-scale appreciative inquiry intervention. You can, however, use the concepts in this chapter to enhance your coaching, consulting, and facilitating practices. Appreciative inquiry can be used in a variety of situations:

- ▶ coaching one-on-one
- ▶ planning strategically
- ▶ planning meetings
- ▶ strengthening relationships
- ▶ reframing problem-solving efforts
- ▶ enhancing decisions
- ▶ generating new ideas
- ▶ training classes
- ▶ benchmarking organizations
- ▶ engaging vendors or customers
- ▶ increasing employee satisfaction
- ▶ launching new project teams.

Organization development practitioners can begin using the appreciative inquiry approach by adding affirmative questions to their coaching, consulting, and facilitating. Get people talking about what interests them most, their ideas, their hopes, and their proudest moments. You will want to practice reframing problem statements and helping people articulate their vision. Here are a several sample questions:

Coaching
- ▶ When have you been most interested and engaged in your work?
- ▶ What do you value most about yourself and your work?

Consulting
- ▶ What is special about this organization?
- ▶ In what ways is the company best in its class?
- ▶ In five years what do you hope will have taken place?

Facilitating
- ▶ If there were no constraints in people, time, and money, what approach would you take?

MIRACLE QUESTION

- ▹ What does a home run in performance look like?
- ▹ What special talents does the team have that will help the company meet its goals in the future?

Appreciative inquiry is a powerful approach to change and OD. It creates an environment that engages and excites people, but it is also very pragmatic and business oriented. By shifting conversations to the affirmative, appreciative inquiry can help businesses grow and improve in ways that inspire those involved. Organization development practitioners should continuously build their knowledge of appreciative inquiry and its wide-ranging applications.

Getting It Done

Create an agenda and plan for using appreciative inquiry at your department's staff meeting. Share the plan with your manager and give appreciative inquiry a try! Use exercise 4-1 as a guide.

Exercise 4-1. Appreciative inquiry staff meeting.

What is the theme for your appreciative inquiry staff meeting conversation?

_____

_____

Here's a reminder of the four phases of the appreciative inquiry 4-D cycle. Create the questions you want to ask for each phase and take notes as to the preparation and actions you will take. You will likely want to break up the phases of the 4-D cycle, tackling one per staff meeting.

Discovery: The OD practitioner conducts appreciative interviews that uncover current best practices, strengths, and strategic capabilities.

_____

_____

Dream: Participants explore and discuss their visions, hopes, ideas, and dreams for the future.

_____

_____

Design: The work done this far is synthesized into a picture or model of what should change.

_____

_____

(continued on page 56)

Exercise 4-1. Appreciative inquiry staff meeting (continued).

Destiny: Participants celebrate what they have created and set actions and projects in motion to make the vision a reality.

_____

_____

In the next chapter, you will learn about a powerful model for facilitating how employees respond to change.

5

Transition Management

· ·

What's Inside This Chapter

In this chapter, you'll learn:

▸ The difference between change and transition
▸ The elements of the Bridges Transition Model
▸ The actions OD practitioners and leaders take to facilitate transition
▸ The Bridges Transition Model in conjunction with change interventions
▸ The considerations for transitioning during nonstop change.

Change and Transition

Change is critical to business success, and is nothing new to OD practitioners, leaders, and managers. They know that in order to remain profitable and competitive, the business must change. The global market and business climate will reward companies that are nimble and responsive to the changing customer wants and needs.

Change is important. Even so, most companies do not invest the time and attention required to ensure that employees transition to changes. This is a shame because managing transitions is easy to do once the management team understands the nature of transition.

Action research and appreciative inquiry are tools used by OD practitioners to help manage and implement organization change. In 1991, William Bridges published an important book called *Managing Transitions* that addressed how people respond to change. No change intervention should be planned and implemented without considering the process people go through to transition. There are many models of personal transition, but the Bridges Transition Model is the most comprehensive and has stood the test of time.

Basic Rule 10

Situations change and people transition. Transition is the process people go through when they react to and adjust to changes.

Change and transition are not the same things. Change is a situation where something transforms. Jobs are added/eliminated. The company merges with a competitor. Health benefits decrease/increase. New software is loaded. Regulatory requirements increase. The company reorganizes.

Transition is the inner process through which people come to terms with a change. Transition is the path people take to react to and get comfortable with change. The process includes letting go of the way things used to be and getting comfortable with the way things are now. Transition is personal. Each individual will transition at a different speed and in a different manner. In an organization, managing transition means helping people to make this process less painful and troublesome.

Basic Rule 11

To successfully implement organizational change, OD practitioners and leaders need to understand and take into account how people transition.

Bridges Transition Model

Transition occurs in three phases as shown in figure 5-1: ending, neutral zone, and new beginning.

Noted

"Unless transition occurs, change will not work. That's what happens when a great idea falls flat." (Bridges, Managing Transitions *[2003])*

Phase 1: Ending

Every transition begins with an ending, a loss. When things change, employees leave behind the way things used to be. They are left searching for a new way to define their reality. Even if the change is perceived as positive, there is some loss and something that is ending. Before you can transition to the new beginning, you must let go of the way that things used to be.

Sometimes people resist giving up ways and practices that have made them successful in the past. They are reluctant to give up what feels comfortable.

Phase 2: Neutral Zone

The neutral zone is a confusing in-between state, when people are on their way to the new beginning. They are no longer in the past, but not yet to the new beginning, either. It's that ambiguous place in the middle that feels murky. They might feel lost. For some, the neutral zone is so full of confusion that getting through it drains their energies. People are driven to get out the neutral zone, and some rush ahead while others retreat into the past. But neither of these approaches is advisable because the neutral zone has a purpose.

Figure 5-1. Bridges Transition Model.

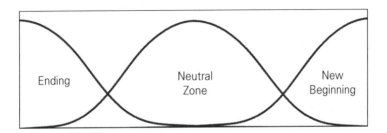

While the neutral zone can be confusing or even distressing, it can also be a very creative place. Time in the neutral zone is not wasted, for this is where the real transformation takes place. The change can continue forward on something close to its own schedule while the transition is being attended to, but if the transition is not dealt with, the change may collapse. People cannot do the things that the new situation requires until they come to grips with what is being asked of them.

Phase 3: New Beginning

The new beginning can only happen after people have let go of the past and spent some time in the neutral zone. In this phase, people accept the reality of the change and start to identify with their new situation.

Some people fail to get through transition because they do not let go of the old ways and make an ending; others fail because they become frightened and confused by the neutral zone and don't stay in it long enough. Some, however, do get through these first two phases of transition, but then freeze when they face the third phase. The new beginning requires people to behave in a new way, and that can be concerning as it tests one's competence and sense of value. Employees will hang back during the final phase of transition if the organization has been known to punish people for mistakes. They will wait to see how others are going to handle the new beginning before jumping in.

Table 5-1 shows what it might look like as people transition. Beside each phase is a list of behaviors you might see.

Table 5-1. Behaviors associated with transition.

Phase of Transition	What It Might Look Like
Ending	Avoidance, disbelief, shock, anger, sabotage, carelessness
Neutral Zone	Detachment, withdrawal, confusion, lack of attentiveness, indifference, creative, risk taking, experimentation, participation
New Beginning	Behavior consistent with the change, focused on purpose, renewed energy, clarity of role, competence

Facilitating Transition

Understanding the transition process is critical for any OD practitioner. Your clients are going to need help to ensure that the changes they launch do not fail. The following are several considerations to build into your change intervention plan for each transition phase.

Think About This

In a marathon, there are thousands of people bunched up behind the starting line. The gun blasts and the folks in the front run. Then slowly the people behind them run, and it takes several minutes before the people in the back of the line begin moving. As the race unfolds, the crowd thins out and the runners come across the finish line a few at a time over a period of hours. Transition is similar. The folks planning the change (usually senior management) start their transition days, weeks, or months ahead of the rest of the organization. By the time the change is rolled out, the senior managers have crossed the transition finish line (new beginning), but the other folks have just started their transition. Some will need extra support, and a few may fall short of the finish line. This is called the *Marathon Effect*. When OD practitioners work with clients, it is important the clients understand and discuss the Marathon Effect to help senior leaders understand how people might be feeling so they can show empathy and support.

▶ Plan (before the change is implemented).

▶ Talk about transition and provide transition management training to your client and the management team. (*Managing Transitions* by Bridges [2003] is an excellent book for this purpose.)

▶ Determine what people are losing: define, in detail, what is ending. Be sure to look at this from several points of view. Who will have to let go of something? Define how behaviors and attitudes will need to change.

▶ Plan and schedule communications. Be sure that the change plan is front loaded with communication to be held in a variety of ways, including announcement meetings, smaller discussion meetings, daily briefings, handouts, and management by walking around.

▶ Design a few quick successes into the change process to boost confidence and momentum. This will help people get through the ambiguous neutral zone.

Ending

▶ Communicate, communicate, and communicate. Err on the side of overcommunication. Explain the need for the change and why the change makes sense now. Communicate the four Ps (Picture, Purpose, Part, Plan). Define and communicate what is and is not changing.

- Mark the ending. One of the reasons people get stuck in endings is that they don't acknowledge what's ending; they hang on to the old ways. Your change intervention should include ways to mark the ending in a respectful and clear way. This might mean letting people take a piece of the old with them as a memento.

- Openly acknowledge losses. If possible, compensate for the losses. What can the organization do to counterbalance the losses?

- Don't be blinded by people who overreact. Everyone's transition is different, so you should ensure that your client and the management team are ready to experience a variety of responses. (Remind them that they have already transitioned.) You will likely see people in varying stages of grief (denial, anger, anxiety, sadness).

Noted

Making sure people understand the four Ps is an excellent way to help them understand changes and get on board. First, you want to describe the picture, or broad vision for the change. Share the desired state in compelling and colorful terms. You want others to get excited about the desired state. Next, you will want to share why this change is needed and is the right thing to do. Be generous with information. Share the condition that led to the decision and why this particular change was preferred over other alternatives. Share the part they will play in the new, desired state and with helping make the change successful. Be inclusive and inspiring. Finally, share the plan, or how the change will be implemented and the various timelines and projects involved. You may also want to review any temporary plans or structures and ensure people know with whom they can talk. Throughout the process of communicating the four Ps, engage the group and encourage questions and concerns.

Neutral Zone
- Communicate the four Ps (Picture, Purpose, Part, Plan).
- Create temporary systems, roles, policies, and processes to help normalize the neutral zone.
- Set realistic productivity targets and expect some slow downs.

- ▷ Provide training and development to increase confidence and competence.
- ▷ Encourage people to share ideas and participate in refining details of the change. The neutral zone can be a very creative time, and you will want to take advantage of this. Encourage experimentation and brainstorming of ideas.
- ▷ Get people involved in the change plan and working together so that the change seems less isolating.

New Beginning

- ▷ Communicate the four Ps (Picture, Purpose, Part, Plan). Ensure that your client and the management team communicate consistently. Be open about setbacks and challenges, and enlist people to be a part of the solution.
- ▷ Celebrate successes, even small ones. Reward people for making their transition.
- ▷ Ensure that temporary policies and structures are replaced with those consistent with the change.
- ▷ Reflect on the change and the transitions that people have made. Measure the effectiveness of the change process and determine any outstanding action items.

Think About This

While nonstop change is an inevitable reality of today's business climate, you can and should guard against the company engaging in trickle change. Trickle change occurs when unexpected smaller changes are announced on a regular basis. Trickle change raises stress levels and slows transition. If possible, wrap smaller changes into a larger change or work with your client to do the upfront work necessary to make the changes simultaneously. Trickle change is particularly a problem when the frequent small changes are job losses or reassignments. It is better to do a larger reorganization and announce all the changes at once than have people worry.

Table 5-2 summarizes the ways you, your client, and the management team can help people transition to change. Use this reference during your next planning meeting.

Table 5-2. How to facilitate transition.

Phase of Transition	Suggestions to Facilitate Transition
Before the change is implemented	Talk about transition, and provide transition training to the management team.
	Define what people will be losing as a result of the change. What is ending?
	Plan communications and front load the change process with open and clear conversations about the change.
	Design a few quick successes into the change process.
Ending	Err on the side of over-communication. Communicate the four Ps (Picture, Purpose, Part, Plan).
	Clarify what is and is not ending.
	Mark the ending.
	Openly acknowledge losses.
Neutral Zone	Communicate the four Ps (Picture, Purpose, Part, Plan).
	Create temporary systems, roles, policies, and processes to help normalize the neutral zone.
	Set realistic productivity targets, and expect some slow downs.
	Provide training and develop skills and competence.
	Encourage experimentation and brainstorming of ideas.
New Beginning	Communicate the four Ps (Picture, Purpose, Part, Plan).
	Be open about setbacks and challenges, and enlist people to help be a part of the solution.
	Celebrate successes, even small ones.
	Ensure that temporary policies and structures are replaced.
	Reflect on and celebrate the accomplished journey.

Responding to Nonstop Change

In today's business climate, change is nonstop. This also means that people are constantly in varying stages of transition. Organization development practitioners can help organizations manage transitions in ever-changing environments:

- ▶ Ensure that your client does not implement needless change. Be cognizant of the toll that transition takes on employees. If the company is in the midst of a significant change process, postpone lesser changes.
- ▶ Help the organization improve its ability to create a contingency plan. Implementing a contingency is less destructive than rolling out an urgent, new plan.
- ▶ Create a culture that embraces change as normal.
- ▶ Frame smaller changes under a larger theme, like continuous improvement.
- ▶ Help your client and the management team build trust. If the employees feel the management team is trustworthy, changes will be less traumatic.
- ▶ Improve the organization's ability to transition by building nimbleness into the structure, processes, roles, and culture.
- ▶ Ensure that your client and the management team are taking care of themselves. They will be less able to help others transition if they are having trouble transitioning. Take care of yourself, too!

Think About This

If a management team is trusted, employees will transition more effectively because they are more likely to believe that the change was needed and well thought out. If the management team is deemed as being untrustworthy, some people will resist the change and their transition will be slower or get stuck. Help your client and the management team improve trustworthiness by coaching them to act with integrity, listen well, understand and consider as many perspectives as possible, and practice candid communication. It also helps when managers seek and appreciate feedback (positive and critical) and keep employees informed.

The Bridges Transition Model is an invaluable tool for OD practitioners. By integrating planning for change and planning for transitions, your change interventions will be more robust and successful. Well-thought-out plans can fail if they do not take into account how people transition. Sharing the model and training your clients and the management team on transition management will improve their ability to implement small departmental changes or changes involving only one person.

Getting It Done

Think about a current change that is affecting you. Look at the Bridges Transition Model and try to diagnose where you are in the transition. What would help you get to the next stage of transition? Do the same exercise again with a co-worker. Use exercise 5-1 as a guide.

Exercise 5-1. Transition management.

List a change:

_____

_____

Here's a reminder of the three phases of transition.

Phase 1: Ending

What you see: Avoidance, disbelief, shock, anger, sabotage, carelessness.

Phase 2: Neutral Zone

What you see: Detachment, withdrawal, confusion, lack of attentiveness, indifference, creative, risk taking, experimentation, participation.

Phase 3: New Beginning

What you see: Behavior consistent with the change, focused on purpose, renewed energy, clarity of role, competence.

What phase of transition are you in?

_____

_____

What actions could you take to help yourself transition to the next phase?

_____

_____

In the next chapter, you will explore internal consulting techniques and learn the skills that you can develop to improve your consulting success.

6

Internal Consulting Techniques

 What's Inside This Chapter

In this chapter, you'll learn:

▶ Critical consulting skills
▶ Several partnership techniques
▶ Typical phases of internal consulting.

Consulting Is Not a Four-Letter Word

Say the word *consulting* and many managers and leaders roll their eyes. They have images of polished folks in blue suits and red ties coming into the company, discharging business rhetoric using fancy graphs, and leaving nothing of significance except a big invoice. Consulting is the brunt of many jokes as evidenced by some magazines' consulting debunking columns.

The concerns are valid because the time and energy spent with consultants is often wasted. As with any profession, there are a few great consultants, many good ones, and a fair amount of individuals who do more damage than good. Why is this?

▶ Anyone can put up a virtual shingle on the Internet and become a consultant.
▶ External consultants often cannot take the time to get to know the organization well enough to provide appropriate advice.

▶ The business world is in love with fads and buzzwords. Leaders get hooked on concepts and programs that may not be the best fit for their organizations (and consultants don't turn down the work). Think total quality management, International Standards Organization, theory of constraints, lean management, balanced scorecard, work out, self-directed teams, business units, and matrix organizations. These are all great practices, but not right for every organization.

▶ The work that the consultant does is often perfectly fine, but the organization does not maintain the changes long enough to realize the full benefit.

These examples relate to external consulting, but can be applied to internal consultants as well. Some companies question the value of their OD function because they question the contribution to the business the internal consulting practice makes. Here are a few common criticisms:

▶ Why does every project need to follow such a long and complex process?

▶ How does this help me meet my department goals?

▶ Why do they not understand what we do?

▶ How do I make sure consultants do not take themselves and their trade too seriously and end up being less influential and effective?

The Core of Consulting

Consulting is a simple process of being an objective third party working with the intent to improve some aspect of business. Organization development practitioners can create a successful and satisfying internal consulting practice by focusing on the three qualities that matter most—competent, catalystic, and partner-oriented—as shown in figure 6-1.

Basic Rule 12
To be a successful internal consultant, it is most important that you be competent, catalystic, and partner-oriented.

A Successful Internal Consultant Is Competent

To be viewed as competent, you will want to excel in functional expertise, business acumen, and communication practices. Your functional area includes OD and might include training or human resources. Your clients want you to have a strong

Figure 6-1. The core of consulting.

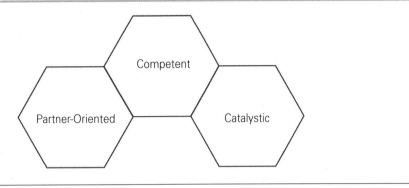

background in OD theory and application, and look to you for ideas about how to improve productivity and results. They likely don't understand the field of OD but they hope you do! You will want to demonstrate that you keep current on advances within the field and participate in local or national professional organizations.

Organization development professionals who struggle to create an effect often do not have business acumen. They spend their time learning the field of OD, but not enough time learning about business. It is difficult to be an effective internal consultant if you don't understand how the business operates, makes money, and measures its success. Organization development practitioners who relate well to leaders and managers will be invited into the business. Those that don't demonstrate business acumen are more likely to be left out.

Being competent also means knowing about your company. Have you created strong relationships with the key players in the organization? Have you taken the time to understand what's going on in the business, and do you know the company's major challenges and opportunities? Have you kept your ear to the ground enough to know why people like/dislike their jobs and the health of the culture? The main advantages an internal consultant has over an external consultant are the relationships and intimate understanding of the organization. To assess and diagnose organization ills and then create effective solutions, you need to know the people and understand the system.

You will also need excellent communication skills. Your clients want you to be the one who knows how to run effective meetings, use email to followup on conversations, produce clear and helpful documents, and give presentations.

Noted

Business acumen is general knowledge about how to run a business. Someone with business acumen understands various aspects of business, including human resources, finance and accounting, information technology, operations, customer service, sales, marketing, procurement, and product development. Business acumen is an umbrella phrase that means someone is sharp with regard to general business management and leadership.

A Successful Internal Consultant Is Catalystic

An OD practitioner can add a lot of value by being a positive catalyst. The term *catalyst* comes from the world of chemistry, but in business it has come to describe a person who accelerates, activates, or increases the rate of reaction to a situation. It's someone who, through proactive dialogue or action, causes an important (and presumably beneficial) event to occur. The right thing, said at the right time, can save an organization or propel it in a new and exciting direction.

Organizations can be dysfunctional. A group of intelligent and well-meaning professionals can go through an entire meeting without one of them acknowledging the problem. Every day, teams plan and implement flawed projects because no one asked the right challenging questions.

Think About This

Catalysts should ensure that they are not being perceived as troublemakers. The qualities that differentiate a catalyst and a troublemaker are intent and focus. First, a catalyst acts and communicates from the genuine intent to be helpful and observant. Troublemakers often thrive on creating a big show and looking good. Catalysts do not share every question or offer every observation. They pick and choose their comments and focus on the situations, issues, or possibilities that are important. If it looks as though the conversation is heading in the right direction, the OD practitioner will let the group get there on its own.

Organization development practitioners are in a great position to be catalysts because they know what's going on in the organization and do not belong to any operational function. They can ask the questions that help clients avoid a disaster. As shown in table 6-1, OD practitioners can learn to become better catalysts by being curious, proactive, observant, and courageous.

▶ *Curiousness:* Show a genuine curiosity toward the business and how each function operates. Ask open-ended questions and listen well. An OD practitioner can play the role of layperson and ask the questions that are often very helpful.

▶ *Proactiveness:* Take the initiative to make things better. Organization development practitioners need to ask about the next steps, making sure people are engaged and in action. It might be that several folks are interested and willing to discuss a situation or opportunity, but no one has taken the initiative to schedule a meeting to get the dialogue rolling. Offer to help people get into action by facilitating or coaching.

▶ *Observancy:* Sometimes the information is all there, but no one has taken the time to make the connections. Make that connection. Notice the verbal and nonverbal signals in meetings and share what you are seeing if you think doing so might help the conversation improve. Share your observations in an objective way.

▶ *Courageousness:* Sometimes the most important message is not being said. Break the ice and help the conversation get real. Being courageous means

Noted

A catalyst is a substance that increases the rate of a chemical reaction but is not consumed in the process. The catalyst is generally used in much smaller amounts than the other chemicals in the reaction. Some of the most common catalysts in everyday life are the platinum, rhodium, and palladium in the catalytic converters on automobiles. Small amounts of these rare and expensive metals speed the conversion of dangerous nitrogen oxides and carbon monoxide into less harmful compounds.

Table 6-1. How to be a catalyst.

To Be a Catalyst...	Try Doing More of This...
Be Curious	Ask open-ended questions about what things mean and how they operate. Act like an outsider, customer, or neophyte, and ask the basic questions that insiders often overlook. Take an interest in understanding intentions and motives behind actions.
Be Proactive	Ask about next steps in meetings. Challenge managers and teams when they seem to overcommit or you sense not everyone is in agreement. Take the initiative to get the right people together to talk about the issues needing discussion. Offer to facilitate. Offer to help managers think through a project plan. Do whatever it takes to get people in action.
Be Observant	Do your homework and review reports and memos from various groups and projects. Make the connection between facts and actions. Notice the topics and behaviors (and perhaps people) that tend to engage or disengage the team. Share your observations in a way that ties into the desired goal.
Be Courageous	Notice the energy and tension in the room, and determine what's not being said. Say it. Ask the tough questions that others might be too fearful to bring up. Notice the differences between water cooler conversations and meeting conversations, and help the group be more inclusive and authentic in meetings.

discussing undiscussables, sharing sensitive information, and being the one to say that perhaps the project should be scrapped.

Encourage others to be catalysts, too. If your organization's culture is candid and collaborative, you may not need to be a catalyst very often because others will share this responsibility. Most work environments are not like this, however, and the OD practitioner's role as catalyst is critical to the success of the business. By being a catalyst, you will make an effect and role model positive traits that will rub off onto others.

A Successful Internal Consultant Is Partner-Oriented

Developing and maintaining productive partnerships is a critical skill for OD practitioners because as internal consultants and coaches, your reputations and relationships matter more than your skills or experiences. Organization development practitioners who fail to connect with or become trusted by their clients have little chance for success. Organization development, like human resources and training, needs to set the example for excellence in how people work together for the benefit of the company. Effective partnerships are an OD practitioner's currency for getting work done.

Most, if not all, OD work is interdependent with other groups or individuals. It takes a team (OD practitioner, client, stakeholders) firing on all cylinders to produce the best results. Effective OD practitioners know that clients and stakeholders are a rich source for ideas and new approaches.

Communication happens on many levels. Some topics are reviewed and discussed in staff meetings. Other information gets sent to employees via email. Sanitized and spun messages are presented to the public. Then there is the dialogue that occurs during informal conversations and lunchtime chats. This last type of information, the informal and unwritten communication, is very important. Emerging concerns, pending decisions, potentially troublesome rumors, and fresh new ideas are most likely to be heard in these outlets first. Organization development practitioners need to develop and maintain excellent relationships with clients and stakeholders to ensure they are part of this communication pipeline.

Working well with others makes work more meaningful and satisfying. When a team works together, the pace of work quickens and the energy is more positive and oriented toward success. Even when faced with significant challenges, a strong and collaborative team can use these challenges to find a creative solution, and not make them the "problem."

Noted

Being a partner is a full-time role. Partners are partners whether they are together or not. They keep each other's needs and goals in mind at all times and represent each other well in conversations in which only one partner is present. You can't be a productive partner in a work session and then badmouth the partner later in the afternoon. That's not partnership, and it is immature and inauthentic.

Partnership Characteristics

Effective partnership helps organizations deal with tough challenges and times of growth and opportunity. Every organization and department can benefit from the coordinated efforts of their talented professionals. Partnership goes beyond cooperation to being a purposeful act of inclusion, collaboration, and co-leadership. Merely being helpful when solicited or asked does not make one an effective partner. Partners seek each other out and proactively involve one another in day-to-day conversations and decisions. Effective partnership emerges from a combination of several traits:

- *Shared purpose:* Partners, by definition, are linked to one another. In an organization, partners need to have a sense that they are striving for the same goal.
- *Shared ownership:* When the OD practitioner, the client, and the stakeholders share ownership of a result or outcome, they are more likely to work together effectively. Co-owning an outcome takes partnership a step beyond cooperation to collaboration.
- *Mutual trust:* Organization development practitioners, clients, and stakeholders who trust each other will partner more effectively. Mutual trust facilitates openness, creativity, and communication. You do not need to agree to develop a trusting and respectful relationship. Often, an appreciation of diverse ideas improves the partnership.
- *Critical thinking:* Without critical thinking, partnership is just small talk. At the heart of collaboration is the act of overcoming problems and creating new ideas. This work occurs best when all parties are engaged, productive, and encouraged to think critically.

Think About This

To improve partnership within a management team, increase the amount and level of critical thinking. Work with your client to re-create the management staff meetings to include more time for collaborative critical thinking. When the management team thinks together, their sense of shared purpose and ownership also improves.

Shared Success and Failure

Organization development practitioners build stronger partnerships when they share the experience of winning and losing. There is nothing like seeing a project through to completion as a team. If the project is a success, celebrating together reinforces the positives of collaboration. When failures occur, huddle together to turn the loss into a win. Sharing successes and failures brings the cycle of partnership full circle.

Effective Inclusion and Communication

Partners talk to each other often and take the initiative to include each other in formative planning and brainstorming conversations.

How do you continuously develop your partnership skills? Organization development practitioners can gauge the type of partner they have been by looking at informal communication practices. How often do your clients stop by and ask for input? How open and lively are conversations with colleagues? Look for examples of successes and failures that illustrate good or poor partnership practices.

Partnership Techniques

Effective OD professionals have learned what it takes to be a great partner. They know that the benefits of effective partnership far outweigh the time and effort expended in creating the relationship. They also know that good partnerships do not simply happen. There are practices that they must put in place and cultivate to increase the benefits of effective partnership.

Resist the Need to Control. If you have a constant need to control situations, people, or conversations, it will undermine effective collaboration with your clients and stakeholders. As an internal consultant and coach, you are not in control nor should you be. Listen and watch for verbal and nonverbal clues that suggest other people are feeling pressured or pushed. Some of the best ways to give up control in a conversation are to ask more open-ended questions and make fewer opinionated statements.

Spend Time With Clients and Stakeholders. Organization development is analytical work, but in a social context. The more time that OD practitioners spend working with clients and stakeholders, the easier and more natural the partnering process will feel. In addition, partners who get together often feel more comfortable asking for input, help, and participation than do those who avoid each other.

Resolve Any Past Partnership Failures. Old conflicts and arguments affect the way people relate to one another. You need to take initiative to resolve any prior relationship issues in order to pave the way for better and more productive collaboration in the future. The benefits of working through and getting past prior problems with clients or stakeholders will make up for the initial discomfort of broaching the topic with them.

Think About This

If you are faced with a peer, client, or stakeholder who does not seem willing to improve the relationship, you can do one of three things. First, you might try a different approach. Can you look at the situation from his or her perspective? Have you isolated the key issues or problems? It may be that what you thought was the problem is not what is actually bothering this person. Second, you are the only person you can control. Even if the other person is hanging on to a grudge, make sure that you continue to act and relate in a manner that is professional and collaborative. If you continue to take the high road, he or she might come around. Third, you can work with others whenever possible. You may still need to conduct business with this person, but when given the choice, it is most productive to work with those who reciprocate.

Communicate on Behalf of Your Clients. Effective communication is one of the most reliable predictors of a healthy partnership. Organization development practitioners and clients who keep one another in the loop and represent one another well in meetings and other conversations are generally great partners. Effective OD practitioners are willing and able to represent their client's interests and needs when that person is not present in staff meetings, brainstorming sessions, and informal conversations.

If You Can't Say Anything Nice, Don't Say Anything At All. Never badmouth anyone in front of others. It never pays to talk badly about others and doing so will break relationships that you will need later. Speak respectfully about others, even if you think ill of them. Organization development practitioners who talk about other people behind their backs end up looking bad themselves. The saying, "What goes around, comes around," applies to workplace relationships. This is not to say that disagreements should be ignored. The best way to deal with a difference of opinion or disagreement is to directly communicate it, in a productive way, to the person involved.

Graciously Share Credit. Partners know that successes come from collaboration and that all players should share the credit. While it may be true that one person's idea was the catalyst for the breakthrough, the overall success was a product of the joint effort.

Know the Needs and Concerns of Clients and Stakeholders. Organization development practitioners will find it is easier to be good partners when they understand the needs and motivations of those with whom they regularly work. Then they are in a position to anticipate needs, warn of emerging problems, and share ideas that will help the organization move forward.

Organization development professionals who practice these partnering techniques will find their jobs easier and more fulfilling. Organization development work is analytical in nature, but it is performed in conversation. Building and maintaining strong partnerships is critical. And for those who endeavor to broader roles with greater responsibility, being a good partner will reflect well on you and improve your promotability and value within the organization.

Phases of Internal Consulting

Internal consulting occurs when the client engages the OD practitioner in a discussion about the business with the intention and expectation that the OD practitioner will objectively assess the situation and offer recommendations. Some say that the reverse is also consulting, but that's incorrect. If an OD practitioner approaches a client, it is advice or coaching until the client engages the OD practitioner in doing something about the situation. This definition also emphasizes that consulting needs to be pulled by the client, not pushed from the OD practitioner. Many great and worthy OD interventions begin as a coaching conversation, but it is important and helpful to distinguish between coaching and consulting. What about when a client asks an OD practitioner to implement a specific solution? That's a project or assignment, not consulting.

Basic Rule 13
When a client engages an OD practitioner in a discussion about the business and asks the OD practitioner to assess the situation and offer recommendations, that's internal consulting.

Here's what a typical internal consulting experience looks like. The client (Bill) makes an appointment with the OD practitioner (Sarah). Bill reviews the situation with Sarah, his ideas, concerns, questions, and thoughts. Sarah actively listens and asks clarifying questions along the way. Bill shares his goal and wonders if Sarah could help make recommendations and pull the project plan and team together. Sarah moves into a contracting conversation with Bill, ensuring she understands the scope and goals of the project, the ideal timeline, who he thinks ought to be involved, and how he would like to see the process unfold. Sarah adds her recommendations about participants, timing, and the needed research, and they come to an agreement.

Sarah begins collecting information about the situation and creating ideas for how to best structure the project and meet the goals. She does a little research and talks to a few OD peers. She meets with the participants to get their ideas and points of view about the project. She shares her initial recommendations with Bill about how the project should be implemented. They discuss the pros and cons of a few potential approaches and come to an agreement on the project plan.

The project team is briefed and the implementation plan is put into action. Sarah monitors the progress of the project and reports to Bill and the team frequently. As the project concludes, Sarah offers a final project report and the team celebrates its success. Sarah and Bill meet a last time to conclude the project. Throughout this process Sarah's role has been as that of the coach, observer, analyst, facilitator, and effectiveness expert.

Noted

Organization development practitioners use consulting techniques: asking questions to collect relevant information, process mapping, assessing communication, identifying barriers, aligning culture, assessing skills, surveying, and facilitating teams.

As shown in figure 6-2, the typical phases of internal consulting look similar to the action research model. Once the project is complete, the client and the OD practitioner review the results and conclude the consulting project. As is the case with coaching, you may find that some consulting projects fit this process while others are more flexible and informal. Even so, you and your client should agree on the goal and ensure that adequate information is collected to devise and implement actions that will be effective and last.

The outcome of internal consulting is usually a new project or set of projects. Sometimes the scope of the consulting project broadens, and it becomes a full-

Figure 6-2. Typical phases of internal consulting.

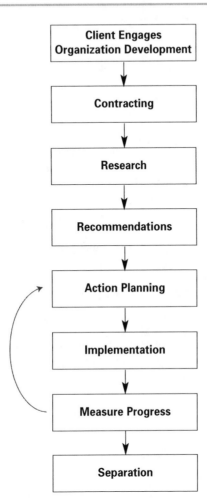

fledged change intervention. Other times the OD practitioner recommends change that would not require a project or intervention (for example, hiring another design engineer). The internal consulting process is a mini version of action research.

Organization development practitioners provide a valuable service to their clients and organizations through effective internal consulting. Talented leaders and managers benefit from an objective perspective and recommendations from an expert in systems thinking and change implementation. The coaching, facilitating, analyzing,

Think About This

Contracting is the process by which the client and the OD practitioner agree on goals, roles, timelines, and communication methods. Organization development practitioners contract in a variety of circumstances, including facilitating, coaching, and consulting. In fact, effective contracting is one of the most important determiners of consulting success. Why? When the goals and expectations are clear, the consultant can focus on the right work and priorities. When the goals and expectations are unclear, time and resources are wasted and the relationship between the client and the OD practitioner may suffer. The OD practitioner will want to ask:

- What are you asking me to produce? What parameters are there regarding the potential recommendations (budget, timeline, restrictions)?
- By when? What interim check-in points should there be?
- Who should I involve?
- Are there any special circumstances I need to be aware of (confidentiality needs, preconceived notions)?
- What is the ultimate goal of this work (specific end result, measures of success)?
- What's the priority of this work relative to other projects?
- Who will I communicate with and which messages do you want to communicate?

and developing you provide during the consulting process keep the project on track and aligned with the desired outcomes. You can build a reputation as an effective internal consultant by focusing on being competent, catalystic, and partner-oriented.

Getting It Done
Use exercise 6-1 to assess your level of partnership with a manager or peer with whom you closely work.

Exercise 6-1. Partnership.

Think of someone with whom you closely work to help you rate yourself on the following partnership traits.

Partnership Traits	This is a strength	I need to work on this
Shared purpose		
Shared ownership		
Mutual trust		
Critical thinking		
Shared success and failure		
Effective inclusion and communication		

In the next chapter, you will learn techniques for facilitating excellent business dialogue.

7

Facilitating Dialogue

What's Inside This Chapter

In this chapter, you'll learn:

▶ The fundamental goal of facilitation
▶ Tips for contracting facilitation projects
▶ Strategies for facilitating conversations
▶ Tips for improving dialogue.

Organization Development Facilitation

To facilitate means to make easier. In business, facilitation refers to improving dialogue. A facilitator helps conversations along and makes it easier for individuals, teams, and groups to achieve their goals. A facilitator keeps conversations on track and moving forward. Facilitators do this in a variety of ways:

▶ help clients plan meetings and define desired outcomes
▶ ask questions that generate understanding
▶ manage over- and under-participation
▶ ask the group to stay on topic
▶ manage time spent discussing a topic

- share and review the agenda and desired outcomes
- listen for and notice what's not being said
- record thoughts and ideas
- increase group energy and enjoyment
- point out areas of commonality and differences
- employ techniques that improve dialogue.

Does a facilitator participate in the content of the meeting or conversation? In general, the answer is no. When an OD practitioner facilitates, he or she acts as an objective third party solely focused on enabling the conversation. That said, many people will both facilitate and participate in meetings. It is common for people to do both, particularly when no facilitator is assigned to run the meeting (like during staff meetings).

Facilitation Is Noble and Important Work

Some OD practitioners turn their nose up at requests for basic facilitation and prefer to work on complex change interventions or executive coaching. Facilitation may not be as glitzy or fancy as some OD work, but it is one of the most useful services you can provide. Look at figure 7-1. The fundamental goal of facilitation is to improve work dialogue. That's the most important objective that the OD practitioner should have when facilitating conversations. Great dialogue improves the way a group thinks, acts, and produces results. Beware of facilitation books or trainings that focus on logistics and organization skills. While arranging the room and creating a clear agenda are important, they pale in comparison to the value of improving dialogue. An effective facilitator can have a significant effect on the results of the group by helping it move forward quickly and with a better overall understanding of what needs to get done. Facilitating great dialogue is a fundamental catalyst to reinvention and success.

Basic Rule 14
The fundamental goal of facilitation is to improve work dialogue.

Figure 7-1. Better dialogue leads to better results.

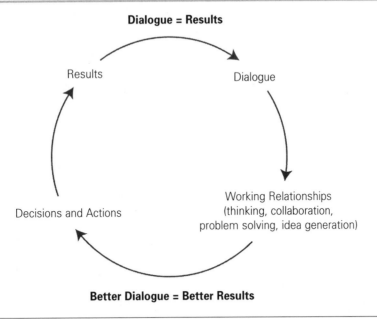

Dialogue = Results

Results

Dialogue

Working Relationships
(thinking, collaboration,
problem solving, idea generation)

Decisions and Actions

Better Dialogue = Better Results

Noted

Facilitation is the promotion of any process and is the reverse of inhibition. Facilitating a meeting or discussion, therefore, should promote good dialogue.

Contracting Considerations

If the focus is on improving dialogue, then the agreement between the OD practitioner and the client needs to acknowledge this. When working with your client to define his or her desired outcomes, ensure that the outcomes are worthy of a meeting. The average 60-minute meeting with 10 participants is very expensive in terms of payroll and time. Table 7-1 shows a few examples of bad and good desired outcomes.

Desired outcomes should reflect the kind of dialogue that is sought and benefits that should come from the discussion. Help your client think about how the time could be best used to move the organization forward.

Table 7-1. Example desired outcomes for meetings.

Ineffective Desired Outcome	Effective Desired Outcome
Everyone is going to provide an update of his or her projects. (Send a memo if the meeting is just for updates; do not waste people's time on a nonparticipative meeting.)	To clarify the new vendor problem, to get everyone's ideas and input for how to achieve production goals, and to narrow down the ideas to a few options worth pursuing further.
I want to present my proposal and get approval. (This desired outcome is too assumptive and does not express a need or desire for input.)	I want to understand the barriers my managers are facing on a day-to-day basis. I would like to come away from this meeting with a better understanding of what is getting in my team's way and their ideas how I can best help them remove or reduce these barriers.

How Organization Development Practitioners Improve Dialogue

Organization development practitioners can help their clients improve results by building the organization's dialogue skills. For each type of facilitation, there are five elements to manage:

1. Has the meeting been well planned? The facilitator should work with the client to ensure that the goals and desired outcome for the meeting are crisp and worthwhile and that the agenda is communicated several days before the meeting.

2. Has communicating the type of dialogue that is sought been successful? Facilitators should share the desired outcomes of the meeting and be clear and specific about the type of participation that is being requested.

3. Have you asked questions that bring forth great dialogue? Facilitators need to ask great questions at the right times to enable excellent dialogue.

4. Did you see and make conversational connections? The facilitator needs to notice when the group is not connecting complementary thoughts or is getting stuck. This requires the ability to listen to the words that are being said and hearing the person's intent, because this is where many disconnects occur. Figure 7-2 shows how messages change as they get passed through the filters (mindset, biases, opinions) of both the sender and the receiver. Is it any wonder why great facilitators are highly valued? Even with the best of intentions, messages can become distorted and confused.

5. What happens next? Don't let a great conversation go to waste! Ensure that the team agrees to next steps, and help the client keep the momentum going.

Figure 7-2. Why we need facilitators.

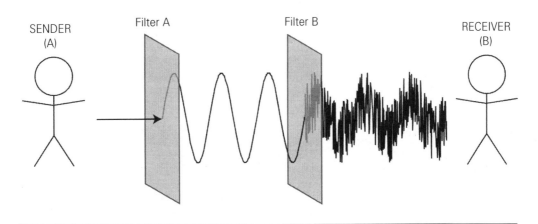

 Think About This

As a facilitator, you may need to become a master translator. Participants from various backgrounds may use different vernacular, and their words won't always connect. In addition, people sometimes mean one thing but say another because of the sensitivity of the topic or their lack of clarity. A facilitator should make observations and suggest connections to improve understanding.

Tips for Facilitators

Some meetings are effective and energizing, but most are not worth the time spent. Great meetings are characterized by great dialogue. Is everyone participating? Are the right questions being asked? The following tips are designed to help OD practitioners improve meeting dialogue for five common meeting types.

 Basic Rule 15

Facilitators improve dialogue by asking great questions.

Think About This

To encourage dialogue, create a handout with a list of questions or words. Put a copy on each person's chair a few minutes before the meeting. Here is a list for you to consider:

- Why...?
- How do we...?
- Who should we involve?
- When do we need it by?
- What about the people?
- What about the technology?
- What about the processes?
- What about the product?
- Where are the barriers?
- Other approaches?
- What would the competition do?
- What do our customers want?
- What do we need to know?
- What's our goal?
- Where will we encounter resistance?
- What are our expectations?
- Where should we focus?
- What's working or not working?
- What would we do if we had no limitations?

Brainstorming Meeting

- ▶ Use when: Your client wants to generate many different ideas.
- ▶ Plan: Email the topic and a list of questions for people to think about. Invite a diverse group of people.
- ▶ Set up for success: Ensure that participants know that their ideas are valued and expected and that any idea is welcome—even those that go against conventional thinking or seem wild.
- ▶ Remember this critical ground rule: Do not spend time criticizing or evaluating ideas. That will only reduce the number and diversity of ideas.

Additional questions that will improve the dialogue:

▶ What are your ideas for how we should/can . . . ?

▶ How would we design this from scratch?

▶ How would the customer want us to approach this?

▶ How would the supplier want us to approach this?

▶ What ideas do you have related to value and profitability?

▶ How would our competitors do this?

▶ What's the most random idea you can think of?

Think About This

There are a lot of fun ways you can improve idea generation during brainstorming meetings. Try giving each person a sticky note and marker. Ask the group members to write down one idea. Ask people to read their ideas aloud as they hand the sticky note to you. Have food and beverages in the room. Scatter magazines and pictures on the table to generate ideas. Ask for the most outrageous ideas first to reduce the resistance to unconventional approaches.

Problem-Solving Meeting

▶ Use when: Your client wants a group of people to solve a problem.

▶ Plan: Email a summary of the problem and the key issues to be resolved. Invite key stakeholders.

▶ Set up for success: Establish the focus of the meeting and determine how much is known about the problem. (The client often thinks more is known, and additional research may be required.) Use a problem-solving process if needed.

▶ Remember this critical ground rule: Be sure to take some time to explore many potential solutions before narrowing them down.

Additional questions that will improve the dialogue:

▶ What are your ideas for how to solve this problem?

▶ Why did this problem occur?

▶ What is the goal or desired state?

- What are the key constraints or barriers to solving this problem?
- What would we do differently if we were to start over from scratch?
- How do our customers want us solve this problem?
- What's the fastest way to solve this problem?
- What's the best solution over the long term?
- How would our competitors do this?
- What's the most random idea you can think of?

Staff Meeting

- Use when: Your client has a regular staff meeting.
- Plan: Ask for topics about which participants want input or ideas. Avoid having the meeting be nothing more than updates.
- Set up for success: Remind participants to focus on items that warrant discussion, and share the topics that require discussion.
- Remember these critical ground rules: Avoid getting bogged down by one topic, unless it is the most important. Don't use the "around the room" approach (you lose a lot of time and may not get to what's important); instead, discuss topics based on interest and importance.

Additional questions that will improve the dialogue:
- What are the key issues for the week?
- What's getting in the way of people doing their best work?
- What new ideas or opportunities would you like to mention?
- What decisions do we need to make at this meeting?
- How can we help each other with current challenges?
- What's the status of key projects? Do modifications need to be made?
- Do we need to begin planning for an emerging need/project?
- How are we doing relative to our goals?
- What's happening in the marketplace that should concern/interest us?
- Would anyone like to get feedback on a project on which he or she is working?

Planning Meeting

- Use when: Your client needs to create or update a plan.
- Plan: Ensure that all attendees know the desired outcome of the meeting and do their homework. Each participant should bring relevant information to the meeting.

Noted

Staff meetings are regular update meetings and are prime targets for improvement.

> Set up for success: Clarify the desired outcome and plan extra time for discussion. (Often, the client underestimates the number of questions and concerns.)

> Remember this critical ground rule: Make sure that the group discusses the "undiscussibles," those thoughts and concerns that people have but may not readily share.

Additional questions that will improve the dialogue:

> What is the scope of this plan?

> What does a home run look like? What's our goal?

> What's the timeframe for this plan? Is this realistic?

> Who are the key stakeholders?

> What are the needs and wants of our customers and suppliers?

> How will we measure plan performance?

> What do we need to consider regarding competition or the marketplace?

> What barriers do we need to plan for and conquer?

> How will we help the organization respond to the changes?

Collaboration Meeting

> Use when: Your client wants to enable an exchange of ideas and feedback on a project, challenge, opportunity, or task.

> Plan: Email the topic, goals, and the type of input you will seek. Invite a diverse group of people.

> Set up for success: Ask people to share their ideas and suggestions succinctly, as you want to hear from everyone. Collaboration conversations should be fluid and flexible. There's no right or wrong way, and the outcome is never predictable.

> Remember these critical ground rules: Do not get defensive! You will receive better ideas and input if you welcome all ideas, even those you disagree with or that are critical of your approach. Show thanks and appreciation.

Additional questions that will improve the dialogue:

- ▸ What information do I need and where can I get it?
- ▸ Where will I face resistance or barriers?
- ▸ How would you approach this?
- ▸ What do you like about this idea/opportunity/project?
- ▸ What alternative approaches can you think of?
- ▸ Who should be involved in this project/task/initiative?
- ▸ What should I do to ensure optimal benefit/value/profitability?
- ▸ Should I be spending time on this?

Think About This

Reinvent staff meetings! The staff meeting is traditionally one of the least effective uses of time. Most staff meetings involve people going around the room and one or two participators hogging most of the time. And yet, most people sit, week after week, through mind-numbing staff meetings that suck the life right out of them.

The Purpose of Collaboration Meetings

Imagine a typical team of seven peers. They each have too much to do and are faced with multiple daily challenges. They have neither the time nor the energy to be creative and proactive. That's where the collaboration meeting comes in. Once a week (instead of the staff meeting), the group gets together for the purpose of providing or seeking input, ideas, and support. Each week, three of the seven team members bring a challenge, problem, or opportunity to the meeting for discussion. For 15 minutes per topic, team members will offer ideas, concerns, thoughts, and feedback. That's not a lot of time, so the team members need to be succinct. Team members rotate bringing topics to the meeting for collaboration, but any member can request to bring a topic to the meeting. The topic to be discussed is totally up to the team member—the department manager should not assign topics. And that's it—peers getting together to collaborate and contribute to each other's success.

Your client might be reluctant to get rid of staff meetings. How would he or she stay informed? When would they talk about the routine stuff? It's all about priorities and time management. Help your client find another, less time-consuming way to stay informed. Their time will be much better spent helping each other move the business forward. They may miss their update meeting at first, but you will find that the dialogue within the team is significantly better—at the meetings and during informal conversations.

If you and your client decide to give collaboration meetings a try, here are a few tips:

- ▶ Facilitate all the meetings or at least the first few meetings, until everyone is trained on the most effective collaboration techniques.
- ▶ Establish a set of ground rules. The list found in *The Skilled Facilitator* by Roger Schwarz (2002) is a good starting point.
- ▶ Focus on solving problems or creating ideas for a current challenge. The point of the collaboration is to help team members improve their ability to get things done, not add new projects.
- ▶ Prepare team members to receive input from their peers by teeing up their topic. They should state the problem/challenge/opportunity, what they know and have done thus far, and their questions for the team. Other than letting folks clarify and build upon ideas, the suggestions should not be defended or shot down. Ensure that people are thanked for their input.
- ▶ Ask your client to commit to trying the collaboration meeting instead of the regular staff meeting for at least two months. It will take a couple meetings to get everyone used to how the meetings work. You will find that the topics being brought into the collaboration meeting get better each week along with the quality of the dialogue.

Do whatever it takes to improve business dialogue! Try a few new techniques, have some fun, but, above all else, take the initiative to ask great questions that fuel the discussion. Facilitation is an important OD service that improves results through enabling conversations that move work forward.

Getting It Done

Think about the next meeting you are scheduled to attend. What questions could you pose that would improve the dialogue at that meeting? Record your ideas here and then give them a try!

_____

_____

In the next chapter, you will learn about the art of great coaching.

8

The Art of Coaching

 What's Inside This Chapter

In this chapter, you'll learn:

▶ The focus of coaching
▶ The four purposes of coaching
▶ Elements in the coaching process
▶ Critical success factors for coaches
▶ How to become a sought-after coach.

The Focus of Coaching

One of the quickest and most effective ways for an OD practitioner to affect the organization is through coaching. Coaching is a service that most OD professionals provide. Coaching yields short-term and long-term payoffs. Helping others achieve their goals boosts results today and builds the organization's skills for tomorrow. Unfortunately, coaching is an underused and poorly understood tool.

Coaching is a client-focused and goal-focused conversation, often held during one-on-one conversations. Coaching can be a catchall phrase for any conversation between two people where the intent is to help. Coaching is a conversation focused on helping another person (the client) move forward relative to his or her goals. Figure 8-1 depicts the focus of coaching.

Noted

Coaching is a conversation that exists to help the client reach his or her goals.

Notice that coaching focuses on the client's goals, hopes, and curiosities. Goals are unmet accomplishments. Hopes and curiosities are the rough material of future goals. In other words, coaching should concentrate on helping the client move forward with something that he or she has a desire to achieve. Coaching is for the benefit of the client. In figure 8-1, the categories that should not be the focus of coaching include what others want, to-do list, and client's failures. For coaching to be helpful, it needs to tie into something that the client wants to accomplish. Topics may be represented in more than one place. For example, a to-do list item may also be one of the client's goals. If it's a goal, then coaching about this topic can be worthwhile.

Many people confuse coaching with advice and other business conversations. If coaching were that broad, this would need to be a much bigger book called *How to*

Figure 8-1. The focus of coaching.

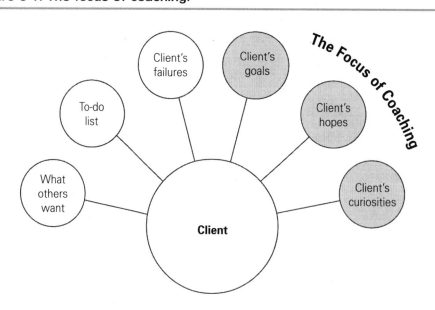

Basic Rule 16

Coaching should focus on the client's goals, hopes, and curiosities.

Communicate. When you give advice, it may or may not be welcome and the conversation is focused on your opinion or perspective. When you provide coaching, the focus is on the other person and the goals they are interested in discussing. The phrase, "Can I give you some coaching?" is rarely followed by coaching.

Coaching is also different from preaching, counseling, and persuading because these conversations come from your point of view and serve your goals, not the client's. Coaching is the exact opposite. A great coach talks little, listens a lot, and facilitates the thinking process of the client. The difference between coaching and a general business conversation is the focus. A conversation can be about anything. Coaching focuses on the client and the goals he or she is trying to accomplish.

The Purpose of Coaching

Coaching, often done one-on-one, is a labor- and time-intensive practice. It ought to provide substantial benefits, right? Coaching in a business setting has four purposes:

1. Coaching should improve client coachability.
2. Coaching should help the client get unstuck.
3. Coaching should enhance client self-awareness.
4. Coaching should facilitate client breakthroughs.

Each time an OD practitioner coaches a client one or more of these purposes should be met. Great coaching sessions might satisfy two, three, or all four purposes.

Basic Rule 17

The four purposes of coaching are to improve client coachability, help the client get unstuck, enhance client self-awareness, and facilitate client breakthroughs.

Coaching Should Improve Client Coachability

To succeed at their goals, clients will need to be highly coachable. What does being coachable mean? Look at coachability from the perspective of a manager. Much of a manager's day is concerned with guiding others, solving problems, and partnering with peers. It is just as important for managers to get coaching that helps them meet their goals. To benefit from coaching, they need to be coachable. Coachability is the degree that you are open to what your environment can offer, or the extent to which you will accept and consider input and ideas.

A manager's success depends on whether he or she is highly coachable when it counts most. Although everyone is coachable some of the time and uncoachable at other times, the most effective managers will be more coachable overall and, most important, during the times when it can make the greatest difference.

Think About This

Begin noticing what coachability and uncoachability look like. Observe how you react to others and how they react to you. Is there an invisible brick wall between you? Why is the wall there? Notice how personality, time of day, and topic affect coachability. In meetings, observe what the meeting leader does that helps or hinders the coachability of the attendees.

Coachability is measured by how well a manager interacts with his or her environment; therefore, it is observable behavior. Coachability is easy to recognize in others (and in ourselves). Table 8-1 shows signs that indicate whether someone is coachable or uncoachable.

When a manager is coachable, there is an open, curious, and relaxed quality to his or her demeanor. Being coachable goes hand in hand with confidence and an ownership for results. Coachable managers display a sense of calm and a focus that allow them to take ideas and process them without feeling the need to defend or rationalize current methods. Highly coachable managers see coaching as a tool to produce better results.

By observing how managers, clients, and peers behave during meetings and work sessions, you will to notice the behavioral cues that signal whether they are coachable. Along with helping your clients improve their coachability, you should endeavor to

Table 8-1. Coachable and uncoachable behaviors.

Coachable	Uncoachable
Not defensive when offered an alternative point of view.	Staunchly defends current decisions, practices, and ideas.
Welcomes ideas and feedback about ways to improve.	Does not listen to suggestions offered by others.
Asks for coaching.	Appears nonreceptive or not interested in coaching.
Reflects on and uses ideas that others offer.	Does not use the ideas that others offer. May be dismissive of others.
Looks for development opportunities, whether in the form of reading, classes, new assignments, or coaching from others.	Does not seek self-development. Does not engage in conversations about self-development.
Is open to acknowledging strengths and weaknesses.	Believes that asking for input is a sign of weakness. Is uncomfortable acknowledging and discussing weaknesses.
Handles failures and setbacks with grace and honesty.	Is defensive and looks for someone to blame. May hide mistakes rather than openly discuss them.
Has confidence and an ownership for results.	Is driven to be right.

improve your coachability. Recognizing when you are being uncoachable is an important step toward improving your ability to grow and be successful.

Coachability is not a condition, like being pregnant; it is a state of mind. People are not inherently coachable or uncoachable. Everyone has moments during which they are coachable and others during which they are not. Saying that someone is not a coachable person unfairly classifies him or her and does not recognize that coachability is a way of being that can be chosen in any given moment.

Noted

Coachability is a state of mind that can be changed in an instant.

Coaching Should Help the Client Get Unstuck

When you are stuck, you feel drained and frustrated. Your brain finds it difficult to get engaged, and your fingers struggle to type the right words. You can be stuck in one area and seemingly effective in another. For example, many professionals can zoom forward with many projects at a time while avoiding and getting nowhere on another project. You might be successful at work, but failing to move forward on your goal to own a company. Sometimes being stuck affects all areas of your work or life because of its importance or connection to your self-esteem. Everyone gets stuck.

The root of the clients' stuckness is often mental and easy to dislodge with the right catalyst. Coaching is a great way to help a client who is bogged down or unable to move a goal or project forward. Clients may be stuck because they are

- ▶ overwhelmed and can't move forward
- ▶ drowning in victim conversations
- ▶ feeling disconnected from goals
- ▶ mentally drained and exhausted
- ▶ suffering from a vague or ill-defined vision
- ▶ not in action
- ▶ trying to do everything
- ▶ uncoachable.

A proactive OD practitioner can help clients get things rolling again. Helping a client get unstuck is a valuable gift that makes a big difference to the success and productivity of your clients and the organization. This type of coaching serves clients' immediate needs and helps build their capability to prevent getting stuck in the future.

Think About This

Create a list of tasks or projects that you want to accomplish, but are having a hard time moving forward. Look at the list of reasons why people get stuck and try to determine which symptom applies to each task or project. Notice any trends?

Coaching Should Enhance Client Self-Awareness

Have you ever worked with a leader like this? Mark is a technically smart leader whom people avoid. Most don't want to talk to Mark nor attend meetings with him. He may know his stuff when it comes to accounting, but he seems to know very little about how relationships work. If you were to coach Mark, one of the greatest gifts you could offer him is to help him see the effect of his communication style.

A lack of self-awareness is not always linked to unknown weaknesses. Sometimes your clients will not be aware of their strengths. Have you worked with a leader who had amazing talents that he or she did not see nor recognize? Some might call this humility, but being unaware of strengths can get in the way of hopes, dreams, and goals.

People who have a good sense of their strengths and weaknesses, who are self-aware, are better able to achieve their goals. One of the purposes of coaching is to help clients become more self-aware so that they can focus their learning and growth where it will make the greatest difference.

Coaching Should Facilitate Client Breakthroughs

Coaching is at its best when it facilitates a breakthrough. Breakthroughs happen when clients let them. Sometimes clients are like sponges, happily soaking in new information. All too often, however, preconceived notions, fears, and the ego shut out the opportunities that they seek. To facilitate breakthroughs, the OD practitioner will want to ask great questions and help the clients increase activities in support of their goal.

Coaching that meets one or more of these purposes will offer value to your clients and be an excellent use of your time. Depending on the client, you may need to begin by building coachability and self-awareness before moving on to facilitating breakthroughs. In other situations, the coaching relationship may begin after you have helped a client get unstuck or produce a breakthrough. You will want to be flexible and observant to determine the type of coaching each client needs.

The Coaching Process

There are two styles of coaching, ad hoc and planned. Coaching may occur in a planned manner, ad hoc, or both. You will find that the ad hoc coaching is often the most productive because it is timely and initiated based on a need or want. Here is an example of ad hoc coaching based on a real situation that lasted less than five minutes, but made a big difference to the client.

Tina walked into Lee's office and asked if he had a few minutes to chat. Tina was struggling to find the perfect person for an open position in her department. It was hard to fill because she thought that the hire needed to come from within the company because of the required specialized knowledge. She had no qualified applicants and was frustrated.

Noted

The term breakthrough means different things to different people. Some reserve the word for describing scientific discoveries and efforts worthy of the Nobel Prize. Others believe they have breakthroughs many times a week. A broad definition of a breakthrough helps generate them. If you thought a breakthrough was something rare, elusive, and unlikely, you would not experience as many. A breakthrough is

- *a moment when someone receives an insight, ah-ha, idea, cognitive snap (relative to the preceding period), or epiphany*
- *progress experienced by an individual or small group*
- *a discontinuous positive change or a leap forward in thinking, action, or results*
- *a change that can be small or large, but there must be an acceleration of progress or sudden insight (transformative vs. incremental).*

Lee: What kind of background are you looking for?

Tina: This position requires analysis, knowledge of the business, proactivity, strong leadership, and . . .

Lee: Does he or she need to be strong in all of these areas? Do other team members have these skills?

Tina: Yes, several have many of these skills and experiences and have worked for the company for a long time. So I suppose the new hire does not need to come into the position with everything.

Lee: Which skills are of highest importance? What about filling this position concerns you most?

Tina: Above all else, I need someone who is a self-starter and who will take charge of the function. What I fear most is not being able to drive improvements fast enough.

Lee: If this is what's most important, why can't the person come from outside the company?

Tina: I guess they can, but I would prefer an internal candidate.

Lee: Okay, but perhaps you should keep revisiting that assumption. Are there other jobs that require similar experiences and skills?

Tina: There are a few jobs that share similar requirements . . .

Lee: Do any of the employees in these positions have the qualities important for this job?

Tina: Perhaps. I don't know.

Lee: Are there employees in the marketing group that have these skills?

Tina: I don't know, I have not thought about them.

Lee: Do you know of any well-regarded employees whose strengths and goals do not match to the work they are doing in their current job?

Tina: Yes, there are a couple people like that . . . hmmm. Wait a minute, I've got it. Thanks. I will chat with you later!

Ad hoc occurs because your client has something on his or her mind that he or she wants to discuss with someone. You are that someone. Coaching can happen any place, and you might facilitate a breakthrough while chatting in the hallway. Organization development practitioners should seize opportunities to offer helpful coaching.

Think About This

You can add a lot of value to the organization by providing ad hoc coaching, but you have to be accessible. Most ad hoc coaching conversations occur spontaneously and because they are convenient. If you load up your schedule with too many meetings and projects, you will not be able to provide quality coaching services. Get up and walk around several times a day to check in with clients, and ask for input on your projects.

Here are a few tips for ensuring you are ready and able to provide ad hoc coaching:

▶ Arrive a few minutes early to meetings.
▶ CBWA a lot (coaching by walking around).
▶ Be available and responsive.
▶ Encourage clients to drop by anytime.
▶ Focus on the client. Coaching should never be about you (unless you are getting the coaching).

The primary distinction between ad hoc coaching and advice is the number of open-ended questions that you ask. Be cognizant and wary of shifting from coaching to advising.

Ad hoc coaching works in many situations, but it is not always adequate. If your client has one or more major goals, then planned coaching is needed. Planned coaching simply means that meetings are planned in advance, and the coach and client follow a logical coaching process. It is important to schedule enough time to have a thorough dialogue. Coaching conversations will be more effective when you and your client agree on the roles discussed in table 8-2.

Table 8-2. Coaching roles.

Coach's Role	Client's Role
Encourage your clients. Reinforce their interest in their goals.	Share his or her goals, desired outcome, and hopes.
Help clients define and clarify goals. What do they want to make happen?	Openly discuss frustrations, problems, setbacks, questions, and successes.
Keep discussions on track and moving.	Share relevant information.
Ask stimulating questions.	Discuss assumptions, opinions, and points of view relative to the goal.
Summarize and clarify discussion topics.	Participate in creating and implementing action plans.
Help clients develop an action plan.	Take ownership of asking for coaching and follow-up.
Offer resources or tools to improve the clients' self-awareness or skills.	Review progress to goals.
Facilitate the clients' coachability.	Be open to exploring new ideas and approaches.
Make agreements about the next steps and follow-up.	Share setbacks or barriers.
Demonstrate a sincere interest in helping clients achieve their goals.	Be highly coachable.

The coaching conversation begins as you ask questions that expand your client's thinking. You want to broaden your client's viewpoint such that he or she may see new possibilities or attack challenges from a different perspective. When done well, your client will leave the coaching conversation feeling energized and ready to conquer his or her goals!

Learning a particular coaching process is not critical. It is more important that you learn the purpose of coaching, develop dialogue skills, and build a reputation as

Think About This

The clients may not make is easy for you to coach instead of giving advice, as they often ask for your opinion. You need to assess whether giving an opinion will be most helpful or if asking a few questions will better service your clients. While it is not the end of the world to offer a suggestion or to say what you would do in a particular situation, it is often better to engage your clients in a dialogue whereby they discover new possibilities. You might compromise by offering both by saying, "I will tell you what I think, but first I'd like to hear why you believe this situation has escalated."

a helpful coach. That said, you might find it helpful to review the common elements found in many coaching processes:

- *Contract with the client:* The coach and client agree to how they will work, confidentiality, meeting frequency, and coaching goals.
- *Define the client's goal(s):* The client's goals are often murky or too broad. The coach helps the client craft specific goals that are inspiring and meaningful.
- *Create a vision for success:* The coach helps the client define what a home run looks like relative to his or her goals. Together they define what success will look like and how they will know when it has been achieved.
- *Determine today's reality relative to the goals:* The client shares the information he or she has collected, current results, and basic assumptions and beliefs about the goal.
- *Diagnose approaches that will help the client meet his or her goals:* The coach offers ideas and options for the client to improve forward momentum. These options are generally not answers, but types of actions and approaches to try.
- *Move past barriers and setbacks:* The coach works with the client to determine what is getting in the way of success and the actions or changes that will improve results.
- *Plan the action and follow-up:* The coach and the client agree on the plan, and the coach follows up and offers assistance as appropriate.

You will notice that these process elements resemble the phases of action planning. Coaching is similar to facilitating a change intervention that is applied to only

Noted

Help your client create goals that are both inspiring and actionable. Goals should be neither too broad nor too specific and should be challenging, but not impossible.

- Too broad and vague: *My goal is to get a promotion (also not very inspiring).*
  Better: *My goal is to develop leadership skills and a reputation of being a great leader such that I can qualify to a broader role in one year.*
- Too low: *My goal is to complete a week of quality training. (That's not a goal, it's a tactic.)*
  Better: *My goal is to ensure I get and stay current with what's state-of-the-art in direct marketing techniques, tools, and philosophies.*
- Not realistic: *My goal is to receive a promotion every year for the next three years.*
  Better: *My goal is to lead my team to being top contributors and being benchmarked by other teams in two years.*

one person. As with action research, an ongoing coaching relationship includes examining results, defining new actions, and then assessing the results again (research—action—research).

Critical Success Factors for Coaches

What separates great coaches from the rest? The answer is more basic than you might think. Here are several critical success factors for coaches:

- ▶ Great coaches are trustworthy.
- ▶ Great coaches act with integrity and follow through on agreements.
- ▶ Great coaches build positive and collaborative relationships with their clients.
- ▶ Great coaches are accessible and available.
- ▶ Great coaches know their stuff. They offer ideas that make a difference.
- ▶ Great coaches know when to be tough. Sometimes the client needs a stronger nudge than others.
- ▶ Great coaches listen well and seek to understand and employ the assistance that their clients need most.
- ▶ Great coaches know that coaching is not about them.
- ▶ Great coaches are catalysts. They are courageous and know the importance of sometimes saying what others have not.

▶ Great coaches are successful in helping clients be more coachable. This opens up many new opportunities.

▶ Great coaches know how to be candid in a manner that will be well received by the client.

▶ Great coaches love facilitating others' success and get a charge out of the proverbial lightbulb.

Professionals from the OD, training, human resources, and management fields possess many of these qualities. Most of these critical success factors also apply to other aspects of helping professions. If you are interested in the field of OD, developing these qualities will serve you in many ways.

What gets in the way of great coaching? Most coaches are intelligent and well meaning, but they aren't all effective. An overreliance on process and protocol can get in the way of the coaching experience and results. If the coach seems more interested in following a specific method or is reluctant to skip steps, the client might lose interest and patience. Problems can also occur when the coach is unavailable for ad hoc coaching. It is important not to overschedule your time and reduce the opportunities you have to coach. There is also a lot to be said for good chemistry. A coach-client relationship will perform better if the chemistry is good. Poor chemistry often leads to the client losing interest in being coached.

Basic Rule 18
Clients seek coaching because it works for them and is a great use of their precious time.

How to Become a Sought-After Coach

Do you want your clients to seek out your coaching? Most OD practitioners endeavor to create the reputation for being a great coach. The ideal situation occurs when coaching is pulled by clients (versus being pushed by coaches). Think about the coaches you have sought throughout your career. What made you want to talk to and spend time with these individuals? Did they know just what to say to help you get unstuck? Could they see through your excuses and help you get back in action? Were they fun to be with? Could they whip out resources on any topic? Your clients will seek your coaching because it is a great use of their time and the experience is positive.

Organization development practitioners offer their time to help the progress of other people. This is the essence of coaching. Coaches never try to replace their client's goals with their own. (This would become advice or counseling.) Intrinsic motivation drives the best coaches to help others learn, grow, and perform. They get a charge out of helping people consider different viewpoints, and enjoy seeing the proverbial lightbulb turn on for people. By helping clients move their work forward, the OD practitioner broadens his or her reach within and effect on the organization.

Being a coach is rewarding, but not always easy. Sometimes you will need to be willing to discuss undiscussables or help uncover unspoken beliefs getting in the way of your client's goals. Your client's beliefs or assumptions may be getting in the way of his or her success. As a coach, you will help him or her clarify what's real and what's not. (And often what's real does not matter as much as what's helpful to believe.) A coach needs to be tough to hold the client accountable for realizing his or her goals. Doing this in a way that does not come across bossy or directive can be tricky. The secret lies in the clarity of your intent and the strength of your relationship with your client.

Noted

Coaching is an art because it is expressive, creative, and highly subjective. While there are methods and practices that build general technique (like in art), the best coaches have learned how to transcend protocol and create an environment where amazing things are possible.

Coaching is more of an art than a science. It is a dialogue that you drive but that is totally focused on the client. Offering nothing but questions can lead to the best answers. Effective coaching produces energy. Whether your client leaves with more energy and excitement depends on the quality of the dialogue. Great dialogue is stimulating, intriguing, and enlightening; and the best coaches make this happen in a seamless and almost magical way.

Getting It Done
Using exercise 8-1, create a list of beliefs that will serve your development of the critical success factors for coaching.

Exercise 8-1. Coaching critical success factors.

Define a list of assumptions and beliefs that would support the following critical success factors for coaches.

Critical Success Factors	Supporting Beliefs
Great coaches are trustworthy.	
Great coaches act with integrity.	
Great coaches build positive and collaborative relationships.	
Great coaches are accessible and available.	
Great coaches know their stuff.	
Great coaches know when to be tough.	
Great coaches listen well and employ the assistance their clients need most.	
Great coaches know that coaching is not about them.	
Great coaches are catalysts.	
Great coaches help clients be more coachable.	
Great coaches know how to be candid and direct.	
Great coaches love facilitating others' success.	

In the next chapter, you will explore coaching techniques.

9

Coaching Techniques

What's Inside This Chapter

In this chapter, you'll learn:

- ▶ Techniques for improving client coachability
- ▶ Ways to help clients get unstuck
- ▶ Methods for improving client self-awareness
- ▶ Techniques for facilitating breakthroughs
- ▶ Socratic Questions
- ▶ Tips for improving your listening skills.

Improving Client Coachability

When your client is being uncoachable, trying to coach him or her can be a waste of time. One of the greatest services an OD practitioner can provide a client is to help him or her be more coachable. To do this you need to have open conversations about coachability and those things, times, or people that trigger uncoachability. By understanding personal triggers, you help the client acknowledge the costs of uncoachability and choose a more productive mindset. Everyone is different, but here are a few examples of uncoachability triggers:

- ▶ Joan became uncoachable when someone questioned her decisions or opinions in front of her manager or peers. She had a strong need to be right, and did not like to be challenged in front of others. Actually, she did not like to be challenged, period.

▶ Kevin did not like to hear ideas or suggestions that affected his tidy existence. He took great pride in planning his time and work. When an idea had the potential to turn his world upside down, even if for the better, he resisted it, regardless of its merit or potential.

▶ Jeremy was uncoachable when overwhelmed with too many tasks. His peers and managers eventually learned that it was best to save ideas and input for another day when Jeremy was not feeling overwhelmed. Unfortunately, he was overwhelmed a lot.

▶ Cathy was a functional snob. She was generally coachable when talking with other professionals in her field of expertise, but quickly became defensive and uncoachable when individuals outside her profession offered suggestions.

▶ Lisa's triggers were time based. She was generally coachable in the morning, but she was less receptive after 3:00 p.m. Her staff learned to catch her first thing in the morning to receive the best response to their ideas.

Basic Rule 19

Your client's coachability is of paramount importance. If he or she is being uncoachable, you should help your client acknowledge this and become more coachable.

Think About This

Everyone encounters circumstances or people that trigger uncoachability. As a coach, you should role model coachability. (Being coachable will also improve your success.) Understanding and recognizing the obstacles that get in the way of your coachability is the first step toward becoming more receptive and, therefore, more successful. It is important for you to be aware of your mood and recognize when you are not feeling coachable. It is better to reschedule a conversation or meeting for another time than be uncoachable and get little from the conversation. Once you become aware of what your triggers are, you can choose a different response and open yourself up to more opportunities for growth.

One purpose of coaching is to improve coachability. In fact, if the client is being uncoachable, your sole focus should be on helping him or her be more coachable. Here are several techniques to improve coachability:

▶ Talk about coachability as a catalyst for success. Clients who believe that being coachable is important to achieving their goals will be more aware of their triggers and more open to coaching.

▶ Ask your client if he or she would prefer to reschedule when you notice that your client is being uncoachable. Share that he or she seems distracted or deep in thought and you'd be happy to come back another time.

▶ Talk openly about triggers. Suggest that clients notice when they feel a wall of resistance, pause, take a deep breath, and decide to let go of the feelings and be more open.

▶ Ask open-ended questions that get the client talking about what is on his or her mind. Tie what you have to what is important to him or her.

▶ Ask follow-up questions that enable the uncoachable person to better understand the ideas and suggestions being offered during the meeting.

▶ Suggest to clients that they should ask for input every day.

▶ Be open about the triggers you see. Share techniques you use to be more coachable.

▶ Schedule coaching conversations at times and in an environment that encourages coachability.

It is critical that you are open with your client about the importance of coachability and goal attainment. This might be the most important coaching you provide your client. It helps to be open and generous with personal examples. The goal is not to be coachable all of the time, as this is unrealistic. It is important to strive to be coachable when it matters most.

Helping Clients Get Unstuck

Coaching should also help clients get unstuck. To do this you will need to recognize when your client is stuck and diagnose the best remedy. Chapter 8 offered several situations that can cause clients to get stuck. Here is the list again, this time with suggestions for how to help your client overcome the causes of being stuck.

Overwhelmed and Can't Move Forward

Clients who feel overwhelmed often lack organization, plans, or processes. It may also be that they have procrastinated or overcommitted themselves and need to bring in extra help. The feeling of being overwhelmed can also be a result of doing work that is not engaging. When you have 10 interesting projects to complete, you feel challenged and excited. When you have 10 uninspiring projects, you feel overwhelmed.

Your clients need to get organized and in action. If there are projects they don't want to do, they should try to renegotiate or find a way they can get excited about the work and get on with it. It might be wise for them to get temporary help if needed.

Drowning in Victim Conversations

A victim conversation gets in the way of progress by giving your client a reason to remain stuck. Here are a few examples of victim statements:

▶ It's not my fault.
▶ I have been trying my hardest.
▶ How could I have predicted this?
▶ It's out of my hands.
▶ This is not my lucky day.

Victim conversations may or may not be true, but that does not matter. They are unhelpful and do not serve your client's goals. While it might be true that he or she could not have predicted a change that caused a setback, dwelling on this is unhelpful. If your client is stuck in a victim conversation, acknowledge the situation, but then transition the conversation toward exploring the beliefs that he or she could adopt that would be helpful in getting things rolling again. One caveat: These suggestions apply to general business situations and not serious mental problems that are better dealt with by a professional therapist.

Basic Rule 20

Victim conversations, although sometimes true, are not helpful and get in the way of goal attainment. Coaches help their clients change their dialogue to be more actionable and empowering.

Think About This

Victim conversations are one of the most common barriers to success. They may even be common in the organization culture (based on assumptions of powerlessness and being affected by the past). Start noticing your own self-talk, and catch yourself thinking about frustrations or goals from a victim's perspective. Reframe your conversations and thinking, and notice what this does for your outlook and your energy level. Victim conversations are draining.

Feeling Disconnected From Goals

Clients may get stuck when their goals are poorly defined or something has changed that affects the goals. Often their day-to-day actions are not supporting their goals, and they eventually lose focus. Help your clients redefine goals that are inspiring and meaningful and then help align their activities to better support achieving the goals. This will also ensure they communicate their goals with others.

Mentally Drained and Exhausted

People have a finite amount of mental energy. There is a difference between making time and taking time to work on goals. Making time means adding on to your to-do list and often leads to mental exhaustion. Taking time means setting aside time to work on projects that matter and removing other tasks from your to-do list. Help your clients make choices about time that ensure they work on the most important tasks and eliminate tasks that are not a great use of their time. Provide coaching that helps them say *no* more often.

Suffering From a Vague or Ill-Defined Vision

A vague vision of the future is hard to create. Examples of vague visions are "provide for my family" or "help the company improve profitability." Help your client crisp up his or her vision by asking open-ended questions that enable him or her to create an actionable vision.

Not in Action

A lack of action is a common reason for being stuck, and is often combined with other barriers. Why is your client not in action? Determine what is getting in the way. Help your client brainstorm a list of potential actions, and then select those that will make the greatest difference. To create a robust list, ask your client to play devil's advocate, and view the situation from different viewpoints. It might be beneficial to facilitate a group brainstorming. Ask for an agreement about when he or she will take each action and follow-up.

Trying to Do Everything

Clients may get stuck because they have failed to enroll others in their goals or ask for support and help. Amazing things can happen when clients share their vision for the future. Help your client get his or her goals into the world and get the process started by which he or she receives input and feedback from others.

Noted

Playing devil's advocate means sharing ideas from the opposing side of the argument.

Uncoachable

Being uncoachable can lead to being stuck because you are not getting the input and ideas you need. In addition to the specific suggestions presented earlier in the chapter, here are several ideas to get clients unstuck:

- ▶ Change their conversations. Conversations create reality, so to improve their reality clients may need to change what they are talking about. To create change, they will want to increase the number and quality of conversations about the change.
- ▶ Tap in to new ideas and talent. It is often helpful to generate additional ideas and perspectives that can reenergize their commitment and enhance their list of potential actions.
- ▶ Put a stake in the ground. Goals can seem unattainable and far away unless there are milestones.
- ▶ Make requests that improve the project's momentum.

Getting stuck is a temporary event and can be relatively harmless with the right coaching to get going again. In time, your clients will learn to recognize when they are stuck and help themselves get moving again. The key to getting unstuck is trying something new—getting into action in a different way. Use table 9-1 to diagnose what's causing your client to be stuck and to identify potential remedies.

Building Client Self-Awareness

Coaches provide a lifelong service to clients when they help the client become more self-aware. Information is power, and leaders who are unaware of their potential derailing factors are powerless to improve. To be most helpful, you will need to recognize the signs that indicate a client's level of self-awareness. Consider these scenarios:

▶ Bob has risen through the ranks and is now in an upper middle management position. Bob's promotions have been a result of his tenure and loyalty to the company. His management and leadership skills are mediocre. His goal is to become a vice president. Bob has a reputation for being emotional and defensive. He does not ask for coaching and becomes uncoachable when offered suggestions in a meeting setting. Bob's managers walk on eggshells around him and do not like working for him. Bob knows that he can get emotional at times, but he does not recognize how poor his reputation is and how this is affecting his goal to become a vice president.

▶ Alexandra means well but she gets too emotional and defensive, particularly around managers higher in the organization chart. She can be articulate when talking one-on-one with her manager or her employees, but is much less effective when challenged by multiple managers or in a group. Alexandra's manager has talked with her about this, and she acknowledges that it happens. She wants to become a more influential well-regarded manager. Alexandra is very frustrated about this and knows that it is harming her reputation. She wants to change but has no idea where to turn.

▶ Lorenzo can drive people crazy. He is impulsive and full of energy. He sees the glass as half empty and has been called "Chicken Little" by co-workers. Even so, Lorenzo is one of the company's best leaders. He pushes himself, his team, and his peers to do their best work by asking lots of questions and being courageous enough to ask the uncomfortable, but obvious, questions during staff meetings. He knows he can be a bit intense and negative at times and generally responds well when others point this out to him. Lorenzo wants to become more facilitative and less pushy. He has asked for coaching and training on several occasions and has used what he has learned.

Table 9-1. Diagnostic suggestions for helping your client get unstuck.

Is Your Client...	Potential Remedies	Your Action Plan
Overwhelmed and can't move forward	Help your client get organized. Help your client get in action. Determine if temporary help is needed.	
Drowning in victim conversations	Help your client acknowledge and transition out of victim conversations. Help your client select and take on better beliefs.	
Feeling disconnected from goals	Help your client redefine goals that are inspiring and meaningful, and then help align activities to better support achieving the goal. Ensure the client communicates goals with others.	
Mentally drained and exhausted	Help your client make better choices about how to spend time. Provide coaching that helps your client say *no* more often.	
Suffering from a vague or ill-defined vision	Help your client crisp up his or her vision by asking open-ended questions that enable him or her to create an actionable vision.	
Not in action	Determine what is getting in the way of action. Help your client brainstorm a list of potential actions and select those that will make the greatest difference. Help your client make requests that will improve the project's momentum.	
Uncoachable	Determine what's triggering the uncoachability. Help your client recognize when he or she is being uncoachable and offer techniques for being more coachable. Help your client redefine success.	

Bob, Alexandra, and Lorenzo have weaknesses that could become derailing factors. Bob has poor self-awareness, but Alexandra and Lorenzo recognize their weaknesses. How should a coach help these and other professionals? These scenarios represent three types of clients: the unaware; the self-aware, but lost; and the self-aware and self-motivated.

Noted

Derailing factors are behavioral habits or skill deficiencies that could endanger success in one's current position or the job he or she covets. A derailing factor is often a strength gone to the extreme, like assertiveness that becomes bossiness or cooperativeness that becomes submissiveness. If you can help your client acknowledge his or her derailing factors, he or she will be in a much better position to reach goals.

Unaware Clients

This is a touchy subject, isn't it? How can a coach help Bob become more self-aware? Bob is also uncoachable much of the time, which makes this a particularly difficult situation. Coaching is likely to be neither welcomed nor effective in Bob's situation for the following reasons:

- ▷ Bob is not being coachable.
- ▷ Bob's goal is not likely the real goal. Most people who covet a title or position are really looking for something else. So to help Bob, it would be important to get him to discuss what his interests really are.
- ▷ Bob's defensiveness is going to get in the way of him hearing about his derailing factor in a constructive manner. Bob needs a proverbial two-by-four effect, which can only come from someone he sees as an authority, like his manager or perhaps a human resources executive.

Self-Aware, But Lost Clients

Alexandra is self-aware, but lost. She knows that her emotional and defensive reactions are getting in the way, and she is motivated to change. However, Alexandra does not know what to do. To help enhance self-awareness, the OD practitioner will need to spend several sessions with Alexandra exploring the root causes of her defensive and emotional reactions. Extensive one-on-one coaching that is candid and supportive will benefit self-aware, but lost clients. Group training classes often don't help because the client is likely playing the role of the victim and the conversation that improves this is not likely to occur in a group. Coaching conversations should focus on the goal and the beliefs and behaviors that best support reaching the goal.

Self-Aware and Self-Motivated Clients

Lorenzo is both self-aware and self-motivated. He seeks coaching and development and is eager to try new approaches. To enhance self-awareness, the coach should offer Lorenzo candid coaching to help him meet his development goals. He will likely be interested in any assessments or classes that will further clarify his style and offer insight.

Does this mean that coaches should not try to coach unaware clients? No! Bob's case is extreme, and most situations are not so difficult. To enhance self-awareness for those in the unaware category, ask lots of open-ended questions and offer self-assessments that nudge the client into being more aware of his or her derailing factors. If the client is receptive to direct feedback, offer an honest and objective assessment of observed behaviors. It is also helpful to clarify the client's goal and ask him or her to determine the beliefs that will support achieving the goal.

Helping clients improve self-awareness means creating the link between their goals and today's reality. Coaches should talk about derailing factors and other development needs in a way that validates that everyone has them. Clients become more self-aware with open and relaxed conversation. It is important that the coaching conversation does not sound like a performance-management conversation because this will get in the way of progress. Knowing derailing factors is a good thing and opens up new possibilities.

Facilitating Breakthroughs

To help clients produce breakthroughs that help them achieve or beat their goals, you should understand the breakthrough catalysts, inhibitors, and mindset.

Breakthrough Catalysts

Breakthroughs occur in various circumstances. Breakthrough catalysts are conditions that often precede and facilitate breakthroughs. This list of common catalysts comes

Noted

When sharing observations, follow the SAR method—describe the situation, action or behavior, and result observed.

- Situation: *You have said that you want to create a more participative environment and you want to encourage your team to share more ideas.*
- Action or behavior: *When you led the staff meeting yesterday, you asked for questions, but your body language said you didn't really want feedback. When no one spoke up, you quickly accepted that there was no feedback.*
- Result observed: *Your staff did not participate in the meeting, and you did not get the benefit of hearing their ideas or concerns.*

from research, survey responses, and narrative examples. There are many potential breakthrough catalysts, and they will vary by individual. Share this list with your clients and ask them to define their common breakthrough catalysts.

Dissonance Experiences. Some breakthroughs happen when people experience cognitive dissonance. Failed attempts, rejections, and embarrassment may cause them to question what they are doing and explore new possibilities. While they do not hope for

Noted

Try using self-assessments to help clients gain self-awareness. If only one individual needs the assessment, there are several online or paper resources you can use. If the entire team could benefit from an assessment, then it might be wise to propose a broader effort. Many coaches use the Myers Briggs Type Indicator or a similar behavioral tendencies assessment. These are excellent for defining general tendencies, but may not point out specific derailing factors. A thorough 360-degree instrument, like the Profiler from The Center For Creative Leadership, will offer specific information. Most professional 360-degree instruments are lengthy and expensive, but they can be worth the cost if you and your clients use the information and follow-up on the feedback received. There is an assessment for every set of skills and topics.

failure to occur, they can use these experiences to progress and enjoy breakthroughs. If they take on a defensive or uncoachable stance, a breakthrough is unlikely.

Taking Action. Getting into action is a great way to create momentum and put goals and intentions into the world—an important step in creating breakthroughs. Many of the breakthrough catalysts are also forms of taking action. Taking action means trying something new, being proactive, or doing what has been put off. Progress suffers when people are reactive.

Noted

Dissonance is a condition of conflict or anxiety resulting from inconsistency between one's beliefs and one's actions or results. For example, an unexpected failure.

Deep Thinking. Some people use mental retreats to generate new ideas, refocus, and tap into their goals. Deep thinking includes mountaintop thinking, playing around with ideas, talking to oneself, and noticing things in a new way.

Coached Nudges. Breakthroughs facilitated by coached nudges are very common. In fact, most breakthroughs occur following worthwhile conversations. (This is why the OD practitioner's role is important to helping clients produce breakthroughs.) When an OD practitioner, peer, friend, manager, or stranger says just what someone needs to hear, it is a special gift. When the clients are open to them, coached nudges can facilitate breakthroughs.

Making Requests. Making requests is perhaps the easiest and fastest way to produce breakthroughs. Mahatma Gandhi said, "If you don't ask, you don't get." It is important to make requests that will make a difference and enable progress. There are two types of requests to consider:

- ▶ Everyday requests—reasonable, modest, helpful
- ▶ Prime requests—a tad beyond what is reasonable, would make a significant difference if granted.

Basic Rule 21

Breakthroughs happen when you let them. Coaching facilitates break-throughs by helping clients become more breakthrough enabled.

Both everyday and prime requests are helpful and should be a regular part of your clients' daily and weekly practices. The more prime requests clients make, the better their chances for exciting breakthroughs. Prime requests will be turned down more often, but the few that are granted will make a disproportionately higher, positive effect.

Think About This

To fully appreciate the power of requests, make five requests every week that are related to your goals. The bigger the request the better. Making requests does not mean you are selfish or greedy. The requests help move your goals forward and increase your contribution to the organization. Once you have tried this for a few weeks and have enjoyed the benefits (maybe breakthroughs), you will be in a better position to coach your clients about how to make requests.

Changing or Realigning the Context. One of the most effective ways to bring about a breakthrough is for your clients to adjust their contexts. In his book, *The Tipping Point*, Malcolm Gladwell (2002) wrote about how the New York City crime rate plummeted in the 1990s, enabled in large part by changes made to the context. Implementing the Broken Windows theory, the city first cleaned up the graffiti on subway cars, and then stopped subway riders from jumping the turnstiles. By changing the look and feel of the subway experience, crimes decreased.

A change in context can have a dramatic effect on perspective. Changing the context might mean creating a workspace that is pleasant and relaxed. The ancient practice of feng shui seeks to align surrounding elements to the goals of each space. Even those who do not follow feng shui will likely acknowledge that a cluttered workspace often accompanies a cluttered mind. Another example of a context change is exploring unknown surroundings to broaden thinking and perspectives. Asking a new group of people to brainstorm solutions to a problem is also a contextual change.

Think About This

Changing the context is an easy and effective way to make new things happen. Is your workspace cluttered? Are you lunching with intelligent people who make you think? When was the last time you asked an industry leader whom you admire for his or her perspective? Is the workspace energizing or depressing? Consider ways to improve your context and keep context in mind when you are coaching your clients.

Incubation or Time Away. Many people say that their best thinking occurs when they take a mental break from working on a problem or goal. There is such a thing as over-thinking something, and taking a break can help clients forget or set aside assumptions and mental sets that might be getting in the way of progress. Perhaps their brains need a rest, and perhaps they are not resting at all. Some believe that the unconscious mind continues to work on a solution while the conscious mind focuses elsewhere. In either case, it is sometimes more fruitful to take a breather!

Breakthrough Inhibitors

Breakthrough catalysts improve conditions for a breakthrough. Breakthrough inhibitors get in the way and make breakthroughs less likely. To take advantage of and have the mental energy to use breakthrough catalysts, your clients need to identify and reduce the number of breakthrough inhibitors getting in their way.

Measure 100 Times, Never Cut. You've heard the saying, "measure twice, cut once," right? That's good advice, but some people take this idea too far. Often called paralysis by analysis, this breakthrough inhibitor gets in the way because, while analysis is action, too much analysis does not lead to forward movement. This is particularly the case for analysis that does not move outside the context (a breakthrough catalyst).

A Focus on Logic. Breakthroughs, by definition, might be a surprise or something unexpected. Therefore, if your clients only do what is logical and familiar, they will reduce the number of possible breakthroughs. Progress follows a path paved by logical and not so logical developments. When collecting and considering ideas and approaches, your clients should not worry about whether something is logical. There will be time to question the viability of the idea, after they've played with the concepts a bit.

A Scarcity Mindset. Some people are less in tune with what's possible. They try one idea and then get discouraged if it does not work. They think it is wrong to make requests to move goals forward. They live in a mental paradigm that is focused on limits and reasons not to branch out and be creative. Their socially constructed reality is one of scarce resources and few possibilities. Clients with this perspective drastically reduce their opportunities for breakthroughs.

Fear. Fear affects everyone at some point. When clients let fear get in the way, they eliminate many possibilities. They should not become reckless, but most fears have nothing to do with impending danger and are likely rooted in a need to be right or save face. In his classic book, *How to Win Friends and Influence People,* Dale Carnegie (1936) suggests that 99 percent of our worries don't come true.

The Self-Fulfilling Prophecy. The self-fulfilling prophecy can be helpful or unhelpful. When clients assume that they will fail and never experience breakthroughs, they are often right. The clients' failures occur not because those were the likely outcomes, but because their brains were tuned for defeat. To combat the negative self-fulfilling prophecy, they need to pay attention to and reprogram their destructive self-talk. By acknowledging the power of the self-fulfilling prophecy, clients can create and employ a more positive model.

No Room at the Mental Inn. Attention is a limited resource. There is a limited amount of information anyone can process at any given time. Most people know this, and yet they don't carve out time to think and create new ideas. There is a difference between making time and taking time. When you make time, you are adding on to the workday and may go beyond your mental energy capacity. When you take time, you are setting time aside in the day, not adding to the workday. When you have no room at the mental inn, you are not available to receive the information that could result in a breakthrough.

Noted

Self-fulfilling prophecy or Pygmalion Effect: Once we establish an expectation, even if it isn't accurate, we tend to act in ways that are consistent with that expectation. Our expectations often determine what becomes reality.

Schools of Thought. People have beliefs and assumptions about how things ought to go. When their schools of thought are limiting and narrowing their range of possibilities, the thoughts get in the way of breakthroughs. To combat this breakthrough inhibitor, the clients need to expand their influences and conversations. Suggest that your clients invite a diverse group of people to the dialogue, try a new approach, or attend a class taught and attended by people they do not know.

You will notice that many of these breakthrough inhibitors can also be good habits in some situations. For example, being logical is often desirable, but a preoccupation with all things logical can get in the way.

Breakthrough Mindset

The breakthrough mindset is a set of beliefs that enables more breakthroughs. By taking on these beliefs, your clients' heads and hearts will be primed for amazing things to happen. Breakthrough habits are the actions that naturally follow when we take on the breakthrough mindset. Those in action and engaged will experience more breakthroughs than the folks who sit back and wait for something to happen. Table 9-2 offers several beliefs that make up the breakthrough mindset and suggested breakthrough habits.

If your clients want to change their results, they need to adjust their beliefs so they are in greater support of their goals. These beliefs support actions aligned with making new things happen. When they practice breakthrough habits, they will experience more breakthroughs and enjoy greater success. These habits are also beneficial for getting unstuck and improving coachability. Give them a try!

Facilitating a breakthrough feels great. Coaches who help their clients recognize breakthrough catalysts and inhibitors, take on a breakthrough mindset, and practice breakthrough habits will enable them to experience surprising successes.

Table 9-2. Beliefs and actions that facilitate breakthroughs.

Breakthrough Mindset	Breakthrough Habits
It is not helpful when I play the victim.	Snap yourself out of funks, poor moods, or bouts of frustration—quickly. Get and stay in action.
Failure and dissonance can lead to progress when I learn from the experience.	Ask for and appreciate opposing views and contrary thoughts.
If my goals are not progressing, I need to get into action (the right actions).	Collect many ideas from various sources. Try new things.
The more I talk about my goals and intentions, the more likely it will be that people will make important connections that help my goals move forward.	Master the art of great dialogue. Broadly share your goals and intentions.
If I am stalled, I might need to change my context or adopt a new paradigm.	Change your context as needed. (If you are stalled, it's needed.) Feed your curiosities!
I need to manage my mental energy.	Take time (not make time) to reflect, relax, and create new ideas.
The more coachable I am, the better the coaching I will receive. The right coaching can make a huge difference.	Ask for and appreciate coaching.
I won't get what I don't ask for.	Make at least five requests related to your goals each week.
My goals are worthy and meaningful and deserve my attention and commitment.	Seek breakthroughs without feeling entitled to them. Make your goals a priority.

Using Socratic Questions

One of the most important OD skills is the ability and motivation to ask great questions. Coaches who use Socratic questions generate rich information that helps clients see their situation. As coaches, OD practitioners can help their clients develop critical thinking and creativity skills. Socratic questions enable coaches to create an intriguing and fruitful dialogue. The Socratic Method, named for the Greek philosopher Socrates, emphasizes the use of thought-provoking questions to promote learning (instead of offering opinions and advice). A well-executed Socratic question stretches the mind and challenges widely held beliefs.

When it comes to coaching, the more questions you ask, the better. If you are the type of person who is comfortable sharing your opinions and ideas, your challenge

Noted

Socrates (469–399 B.C.) was a fifth century Athenian philosopher known for his interactive methods of teaching, examination of the concept of piety, adherence to civil obedience, and inquiries into the basis of virtue. He is best remembered for his ultimate act of civil obedience, administering his own death sentence by drinking hemlock after having been convicted of corrupting the youth of Athens and undermining religion.

He left no literature of his own, so everything that is known about Socrates has been gleaned from the writings of his contemporaries and his students. As a youth, his interests leaned toward scientific theories, and he may have practiced his father's art of sculpture. He later distinguished himself as a courageous soldier in the Peloponnesian War between Athens and Sparta. After becoming politically involved with opponents of a democratic government in the years after the war, Socrates retired to become a stonemason, husband, and father. It was only after his own father, Sophroniscus, left him an inheritance that Socrates had the financial security necessary to devote his life to teaching and philosophical dialogue.

The approach to philosophy espoused by Socrates was based upon four pillars: ironic modesty, the questioning of habit, a devotion to truth, and dispassionate reason. The dialogues for which he is so well known had as their goal the understanding and attainment of virtue, which is defined as excellence, skill, or artistry. To that end, Socrates taught by engaging his students in dialogue and questioning widely held beliefs and doctrines. He believed that it was necessary to acknowledge our own ignorance in order to take the first step toward genuine knowledge and, in defense of the actions that brought upon him a sentence of death, uttered the timeless assertion, "The unexamined life is not worth living."

will be to resist giving advice. Advice may be helpful at times, but the most effective coaching will facilitate your client's thinking process. To do this, try using Socratic questions.

Socratic questions are probing and open-ended. You can use these questions in any situation. Inquiry creates change and is the cornerstone of coaching (and many OD practices) because it helps clients think and solve problems creatively. Socratic questions will also help your clients clarify what they understand and in which areas they need more information. Throughout your coaching session, these questions will bring new strategies and ideas. When you ask great questions, you create an exciting dialogue that your client will find intrinsically motivating.

Questions That Clarify Your Client's Goals

▶ What would you like to see happen?

▶ How would you like the change to occur?

▶ Why do you want this change?

▶ What do you want to change?

▶ What will things look like in a year if everything goes as planned?

▶ What are the consequences of not changing?

Questions That Clarify Your Client's Intent or Motives

▶ Why do you want this particular outcome?

▶ Why do you say that?

▶ How will you benefit?

▶ Why is this change important?

▶ What gave you this idea?

▶ Who will benefit from this change?

Questions to Ensure Your Client's Goals Are Aligned for Success

▶ How does this help you achieve your goal?

▶ Where will this goal lead?

▶ What does this mean to you?

▶ What do you already know about this approach?

▶ How does this change affect the other aspects of the organization?

▶ What do you think will happen once the change is in place?

Questions to Uncover Your Client's Basic Assumptions

▶ What are your assumptions about . . . ?

▶ What other assumptions could also be valid?

▶ How do you know that what you believe is true?

▶ Why do you believe this change is needed?

▶ What does your peer/manager/team think about this situation?

▶ What would happen if . . . ?

▶ What is the significance of your assumption?

▶ Why do you think I asked you this question?

▶ Why is this question difficult to answer?

Questions to Discover if Your Client Has Enough Information

- ▸ What information do you need to understand about this situation?
- ▸ What generalizations have you made?
- ▸ What data has been reviewed?
- ▸ How do you know that . . . ?
- ▸ Why is this situation occurring?
- ▸ What can you do to be sure?
- ▸ Have you seen a situation similar to this before?
- ▸ What is the cause?
- ▸ What verification is there to support your claim?

Questions to Help Your Client See Other Points of View

- ▸ What might be an alternative approach?
- ▸ Is there another way to view this situation?
- ▸ What are the pros and cons of your approach?
- ▸ How is this similar to or different from the way you have approached this in the past?
- ▸ What is the opposite point of view?
- ▸ What would an opponent of the idea say?
- ▸ What would your customers say?
- ▸ How would your competitors approach this?
- ▸ What other ideas have you researched?
- ▸ How does this affect . . . ?

Socratic questions improve your ability to remain objective by facilitating self-discovery. They also serve to expand your client's analysis of the situation and increase the number and quality of possibilities he or she considers. Using Socratic questions increases the energy of the dialogue and improves your client's learning and discovery. Organization development practitioners use Socratic questions in a variety of OD practices, including coaching, change interventions, facilitating, and consulting.

Active Listening

Organization development practitioners need to be excellent listeners and should develop the ability to listen actively. Active listening is critical because so much of your work depends on clear communications and good relationships. It is a way of listening and responding to your clients and stakeholders that improves mutual understanding. Many people are poor listeners. They get distracted, talk too much, and think about what they are going to say next when they should be listening. They assume that they know what the other person is going to say and tune that person out. It can be difficult to take the time and energy to listen actively, but as an OD professional, the rewards are worth the effort. You are listening actively when you:

- Demonstrate a sincere desire to pay attention to the other person (instead of mentally practicing what you are going to say next).
- Commit to being coachable and open with the information being received from the other person.
- Relate to the other person's perspective and empathize with his or her point of view.
- Seek to understand the other person.
- Pay attention and aren't distracted by other things in the environment.
- Ensure you have interpreted it as intended through feedback, confirming, restating, or paraphrasing.
- Reflect on what the other person is saying.
- Synthesize the information, emotion, and feelings to improve understanding.
- Clarify the information by asking questions and probing.
- Validate perceptions and assumptions.
- Let the other person talk.

Noted

Active listening is the practice of showing a client or co-worker that you are listening and interested in what he or she has to say. This involves giving them your full attention through verbal and nonverbal encouragement and validation.

Many people let full calendars, long to-do lists, stress, and their natural behavioral tendencies get in the way of their ability to actively listen. To get in the habit of listening actively, try these tips:

- Give the other person good eye contact; don't let your eyes roam around the room.
- Take notes, but don't look at other papers or reports.

- ▶ Let the other person talk, and do not worry about filling the lulls in between sentences.
- ▶ Ask clarifying questions.
- ▶ Put yourself in the other person's shoes mentally.
- ▶ Respond to what the other person is saying so that he or she can tell you are listening.
- ▶ Eliminate distractions like phone, pager, and email pings.

Active listening is a habit that you can develop. Being a great listener benefits OD practitioners by reducing misunderstandings, improving information accuracy, and ensuring that they have complete information from which to work. Clients and stakeholders will open up more to people who listen well.

Think About This

To test and develop your active listening skills, ask only questions, and let other people do most of the talking for one week. Leave 15 seconds in between the other person's words and your next comment. Practice zoning in on other people and intently listening to them. Pretend you are fascinated with what they are saying, and imagine that their words hold the key to an intriguing puzzle. Guess what, they do!

These techniques focus on what matters most in a coaching situation. To be of greatest help, establish a healthy, effective, and proactive relationship with your client. By helping clients identify and get past barriers and generate new possibilities, they will move their goals forward in ways they would have not achieved without your valuable help.

Getting It Done

You have covered a lot of ground in this chapter. Refer to table 9-2, and try taking on the breakthrough mindset and practicing the breakthrough habits for two weeks. Notice how this changes your results and your relationship with your goals. Then you will be ready to suggest the same for your clients.

In the next chapter, you will explore several OD tools and methods that are beyond the basics.

10

Beyond the Basics

What's Inside This Chapter

In this chapter, you'll learn:

- ▶ Components of a succession plan
- ▶ About Open Space Technology
- ▶ Elements of a Future Search Conference
- ▶ Techniques for assessing organization culture.

The previous chapters focused on the most common and fundamental OD practices and methods. The decision of what to include was difficult as the field is very broad. Choices were made based on the results of the job description assessment summarized in chapter 2. In this chapter, you will be introduced to four practices that are important for OD practitioners to learn, but that are beyond the basics.

Succession Planning

For a company to be optimally successful, it needs to have the right people in the right roles. Finding, grooming, and keeping great talent is a strategic advantage. Succession planning has always been important, but as the baby boomers retire it will become even more vital. Fewer replacements will be available to fill important middle and senior level jobs. In 2003 over one-third of the federal workforce was eligible for retirement. Companies that have reduced the number of management layers will find that they have less people to draw from for promotions. An effective succession plan can help organizations build talent and prepare for turnover. In some organizations, human resources professionals produce and manage the succession plan. In others, OD or training professionals do this work. Often, human resources, training, and OD professionals partner to ensure that skill gaps are addressed.

Basic Rule 22

Organizations need an effective succession plan to prepare for turnover and ensure their bench strength.

Succession planning establishes a set of practices for hiring, developing, and promoting top talent. A succession plan should address middle and senior level management and other key positions. An effective plan will ensure that potential successors are ready to take on a broader role within a reasonable period of time (usually one to four years, with more time needed for senior positions). The succession plan should consider organization values, such as diversity, inclusion, and strategic competencies. To create a succession plan:

- ▶ Select key positions to be included in the succession plan.
- ▶ Define current and future responsibilities, skills, and experiences required for each position.
- ▶ Identify potential successors and their level of readiness.
- ▶ Identify gaps in current employee and candidate competency levels.
- ▶ Create and implement individual development plans.
- ▶ Develop a recruitment plan for positions without adequate potential successors.
- ▶ Develop individual development plans for employees.
- ▶ Develop a communication strategy.
- ▶ Develop and implement coaching and mentoring programs.
- ▶ Assist with leadership transition and development.
- ▶ Develop an evaluation plan for succession management.

Well-planned and implemented succession plans improve retention and protect against devastating setbacks that can be caused by vacancies in key positions. They also improve the value of development efforts by directly tying them to the needs of the individual and the organization.

Succession plans require the participation and commitment of senior management. Senior management must be committed to developing potential successors (sometimes called high potentials) and to promoting from the pool of potential successors whenever possible and appropriate. Senior management must also be involved in establishing which skills and experiences are most important to the company.

Think About This

There are differing schools of thought about the confidentiality of the names on a succession plan. It is optimal to be open with succession plan participants about the positions they might be considered for and the development that is required in order for them to be a competitive candidate for the position. Those who have not been identified as a potential successor might get upset, but you should help your clients turn this into an opportunity to be open with these individuals and provide them with goals they can achieve to improve their standing.

Open Space Technology

In 1985, Harrison Owen created Open Space Technology. He noticed that at traditional large-group meetings, the participants' favorite part seemed to be the coffee break (despite all the planning and preparation that went into the meeting). Tired of working hard to prepare a meeting only to have the unprepared parts be remembered, he decided to bring elements of coffee break discussion into the meeting. Inspired by the social organization of tribal West Africa, Owen created a meeting structure that revolved around a large circle of self-organized participants. As he tweaked the meeting design, preparation time went down and participation went up.

Open Space Technology allows a diverse group of people to create energizing and productive meetings. Open Space meetings ensure that all issues and ideas that people are willing to raise are discussed. There is a natural selection process that occurs because people can choose to join any discussion and may leave and go to another discussion (or out of the room completely) at any time. Throughout the meeting process, the most interesting or important topics become clear because they receive energy and participation. Conversations can become very intense and committed.

According to Owen, Open Space operates under four principles:

1. Whoever comes are the right people.
2. Whatever happens is the only thing that could have happened.
3. Whenever it starts is the right time.
4. Whenever it's over it's over.

Open Space also operates under one law. The law is known as the Law of Two Feet: If at a time you find yourself in any situation where you are neither learning nor contributing, use your two feet and move to some place more to your liking.

Basic Rule 23

Open Space Technology is an exceptional method for uncovering and addressing the issues and ideas that are important to employees.

In an Open Space meeting, there is a big circle of chairs in the middle of the room and several smaller groupings of chairs around the periphery. An accessible blank wall is used to post meeting locations, notes, and results. The group is welcomed and a facilitator reviews the process for the day and the theme of the discussion. The facilitator invites participants to share meeting topics (which are areas of concern, problems, ideas, or opportunities) via written communications. A meeting time and place are indicated for each suggested topic. The facilitator collects and posts topics until there are no more offered by the participants. The large group then breaks up, reviews the topics on the wall, and selects which meeting(s) to attend. Meetings take place and notes are collected and posted on the wall. Topics that are similar are put together, and the next steps are recorded for each topic. The group reflects on the meeting by returning to the large circle of chairs and sharing their experiences and feelings about the process. All of the results are collected and create a larger document that is available to meeting participants and others. Meetings of one day or less will be light on action steps, but meetings of two days or more will offer more details and action planning.

Open Space Technology is best used in a situation where there is a complexity of elements and a need for a quick resolution and people have diverse and passionate ideas. It should not be used when decisions have already been made or if the management team is not open to a wide variety of possible changes. The outcome of Open Space cannot be determined. Although OD practitioners should not attempt to facilitate a large Open Space meeting without training, you can use the idea generation and discussion techniques in smaller groups.

Think About This

One appeal of the Open Space Technology approach is that anyone can suggest a topic (related to the theme). Try using a mini version of Open Space at your next team meeting. Create a theme, invite topics, post them on the wall, and let the conversations begin. You will need to make some modifications if your group is small (under 10), and you will need to expand the time of your meeting to allow many topics to be discussed.

The Future Search Conference

In his book, *Discovering Common Ground,* OD pioneer Marvin Weisbord (1993) wrote that deep and long-lasting change is more likely if you get the whole system in the room. Marvin Weisbord and Sandra Janoff created Future Search as a way to transform planning meetings into conferences that excite, engage, and reinforce common values and produce superior planning. The meeting design enables greater creativity and consensus among a diverse audience that is not possible using traditional meeting formats.

The Future Search Conference design is based on three assumptions. The first assumption is that because change is so rapid, individuals in organizations need more face-to-face interaction to make good strategic decisions. The second assumption is that successful strategies come from envisioning preferred futures. And the third assumption is that people will commit to plans they have participated in creating.

Future Search enables an organization to quickly plan a new future (strategic planning) and transform its capabilities. The group size is generally between 25 and 100 stakeholders. Having either the whole system or representatives of the whole system is critical. The Future Search meeting takes three days and the goal is to

Basic Rule 24

The Future Search Conference works by getting the whole system in the meeting and engaging in conversation about an ideal future and strategies for moving toward it.

develop a common view of the desired future. The meeting is also very task and action oriented, and the last day is devoted to making commitments and creating detailed action plans.

There are four principles that form the foundation of the Future Search Conference:

1. Get the whole system in the room. Invite all stakeholders or a representation of all stakeholder groups.
2. Explore an ideal future, in a broad sense, before drilling down and problem solving.
3. Focus on common ground.
4. Create a bias toward action.

The Future Search Conference is self-managed, and it is up to the participants to determine the discussion topics, manage time, and create action plans. The facilitator establishes the structure, manages the broader processes, and ensures participation. Planning for the Future Search meeting is quite extensive, and an OD practitioner should not attempt to do this without specific training.

Organization Culture

Organization development professionals should regard themselves as the caretakers of their organization's culture. The leaders and managers often have the greatest influence on the culture, but OD practitioners are in the best position to assess and understand the corporate culture and create a plan for its improvement.

Every company has a culture, and many have more than one. Despite what some leaders hope, an organization culture is not equal to the pithy mission statements created at offsite meetings. In his book, *Organizational Culture and Leadership*, Edgar Schein (1992) defined culture as "a pattern of basic assumptions—invented, discovered, or developed by a given group as it learns to cope with its problems of external adaptation and internal integration—that has worked well enough to be considered

Basic Rule 25

Organization culture drives actions and must be considered when planning and implementing change.

valid and, therefore, to be taught to new members as the correct way to perceive, think, and feel in relation to those problems." Any group that has worked together to establish a set of basic assumptions has its own culture. Another definition of culture, from *An Experiential Approach to Organization Development,* by Donald Harvey and Donald Brown (1988), is that "Culture is a system of shared values and beliefs which interact with an organization's people, structure, and systems to produce behavioral norms (the way things are done around here)."

Cultural elements may be strong or weak. Stability of leadership, strength of convictions, and a sense of urgency will strengthen cultural elements. Conversely, new or changing leadership and an absence of important or urgent work will weaken cultural elements. This also means that change will likely take time unless changes are paramount on people's minds. For example, after the terrorist attack against the United States on September 11, 2001, many travel companies needed to reinvent their businesses to survive. New assumptions and beliefs quickly replaced previous cultural elements because of the urgency and importance of the business challenge.

Culture drives actions, and both change over time (often slowly). Organization cultures need to change more rapidly than ever to keep up with business changes. A culture that worked well five years ago may not support the needs of the business or its employees today. In today's competitive and global business environments, a high-performing culture can be a strategic advantage.

How do you determine your company's culture? As a starting point, answer these questions:

- ▶ Which behaviors and actions are reinforced and rewarded?
- ▶ What is important to leaders and managers?
- ▶ Who gets promoted?
- ▶ What type of individual fits and does not fit within the organization?
- ▶ How do employees describe the work environment?
- ▶ Why do people leave the company?
- ▶ What do people celebrate?

- ▶ How would you describe the company's competitive advantage?
- ▶ Is open communication encouraged or discouraged?
- ▶ What's the predominant style of management?
- ▶ Which is more important, individuality or compliance?
- ▶ How is talent acknowledged?
- ▶ How inclusive is the environment?
- ▶ How does the culture react to change?

For each question, dig beyond what's printed in the employee manual and take a look at what's really going on in the organization. Think about the assumptions and beliefs that underlie leadership behaviors and practices. Cultural elements can be both conscious and unconscious, so it is not enough just to ask people to define the culture. You will need to be a keen observer to objectively discern some aspects of the culture. Often, someone new to the organization or an outside consultant will assess the culture more fully.

There may be many interpretations of what a high-performing culture looks like. Can an efficient culture built on the assumptions and values of the industrial revolution (directive, workers cannot be trusted, people as machines, people need to be watched, people are motivated by extrinsic rewards) be considered high performing if it meets the organization's goals? Perhaps it can, but one could also argue that the productivity could be even higher if the culture was improved to reflect current behavioral sciences theories and models. That said, a high performance culture typically contains these elements:

- ▶ enlivens intrinsic motivation
- ▶ allows enough flexibility to allow people to do their best work
- ▶ encourages collaboration and partnership
- ▶ is results oriented
- ▶ is inclusive
- ▶ encourages play and creativity
- ▶ values talent
- ▶ promotes trustworthiness
- ▶ builds business acumen
- ▶ enables transition
- ▶ reinforces participation and engagement.

Think About This

If you determine how the organization culture ought to change, you will need to ensure that all systemic elements are supporting the changes. Changing the culture means changing beliefs, assumptions, actions, and practices. How should your goals for the culture affect hiring practices? How should your goals for the culture affect leadership and management practices? One technique you can use is to build a culture filter. Create a list of desired cultural elements (like the one provided earlier in this section), and compare it to systemic elements and decisions. This practice will help you and your clients make better decisions and improve the organization's culture.

Why would a company be interested in analyzing its culture? If the organization wants to maximize its ability to attain its strategic objectives, it must know if the prevailing culture supports and drives the actions necessary to achieve its strategic goals. Cultural assessment can enable a company to analyze the gap between the current and desired culture. Developing a picture of the ideal and then taking a realistic look at the gaps is vital information that can be used to design interventions to close the gaps and bring specific elements of culture into line. If your competitive environment is changing fast, your organizational culture may also need to change. However, you may only need to change some of the practices and secondary values while keeping a few precious and non-negotiable core values intact. Often an objective assessment tool focuses on a limited number of elements of culture that need to change, rather than embarking on the futile attempt to change the entire culture.

The list of topics for this chapter could have continued, but these four were selected for their importance and prevalence in the field of OD.

Getting It Done

Select one of the topics discussed in this chapter for further reading or research. See the Additional Resources section to get you started.

In the next chapter you will learn the elements that tie most OD practices together.

11

Continuing Your
Exploration of
Organization Development

▪ ▪

What's Inside This Chapter

In this chapter, you'll learn:

▶ Elements that underlie most OD practices

▶ Suggestions for continuing your exploration of OD.

There's a lot to learn about OD, and this book covered many of the basics. Organization development is an exciting field of work that helps organizations, teams, and individuals do their best work. Each chapter explored various techniques the OD practitioner performs. Have you noticed the recurring themes? Most OD practices, methods, and models share these elements:

▶ *Relationships reign:* Your clients are your partners and together you can do great work. Developing and maintaining positive and collaborative relationships are critical for all OD practitioners. Successful OD professionals build lasting and trusting relationships. They are a pleasure to work with and add value to the organization.

▶ *Organization development exists to help the business succeed:* Organization development is a results-oriented function. While much of the work involves building human capability and improving the organization's culture, this work is done with the end goal of improved productivity and results in mind. It just so happens that when people are at their best, results soar.

▶ *Analysis is front and center:* Organization development is an analytical field. Whether orchestrating a large change intervention or coaching an individual leader, the OD practitioner seeks to understand current conditions and how changes affect results. The action research paradigm (research—action—research) underlies most OD projects.

▶ *Inquiry creates change:* The OD practitioners encourage inquiry in most every project and task they tackle. Inquiry engages the mind and gives birth to exciting, new possibilities.

▶ *Change should be planned:* The discipline of planning is critical to OD work. Organization development practitioners help clients implement well-thought-out change projects and initiatives that consider all aspects of the system.

▶ *Concern with the system:* Whether working with a design team on an organization realignment or a staff team on a brainstorming session, the OD practitioners keep the organization's systemic elements in mind. They know that it is better to consider all parts of the system upfront for the best results.

▶ *Goals should be inspiring:* Organization development does not exist to perpetuate the status quo. Organization development practitioners exist to help make possibilities realities. In all aspects of their work, OD professionals help their clients define and move toward exciting visions of the future.

▶ *Culture enables or hinders progress:* Organization development practitioners help clients understand, consider, and develop the organization culture.

▶ *Values guide every intervention:* Organization development values run through all OD practices and enable OD practitioners to ensure that their work is focused and will yield maximum benefits.

Additional Development Suggestions

The OD work you do is important and can make a big difference. The topics covered in this book are just the beginning! Here are a few ways you can continue to develop your OD knowledge, skills, and experiences:

▶ Select one book from the Additional Resources section to read each month.

▶ Join the local or national Organization Development Network to keep up with what's cutting edge in the field of OD. Participate in local and national meetings and events.

▶ Attend professional training courses and certification programs. The interaction with your peers and instructors will build your network and broaden your skills and perspectives.

▶ Pursue a degree in OD. This is particularly important if you aspire to become a senior level OD practitioner.

▶ Practice OD. The information provided in this book should have given you several ideas for projects.

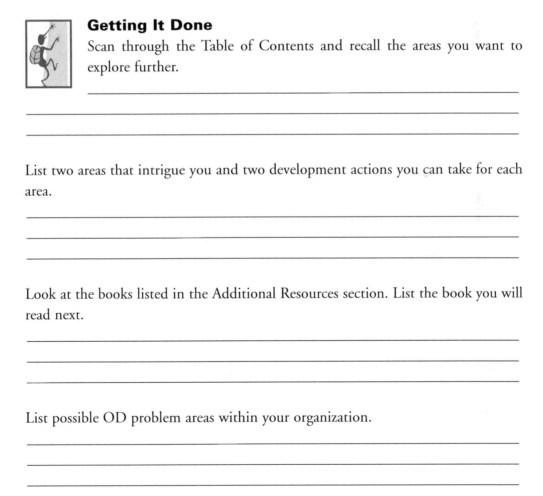

Getting It Done

Scan through the Table of Contents and recall the areas you want to explore further.

_____

_____

_____

List two areas that intrigue you and two development actions you can take for each area.

_____

_____

_____

Look at the books listed in the Additional Resources section. List the book you will read next.

_____

_____

_____

List possible OD problem areas within your organization.

_____

_____

_____

Choose one, and create a project description. Share this with your manager or client.

_____

_____

_____

Best wishes from one OD practitioner to another!

References

Bridges, W. (1991). *Managing Transitions.* Philadelphia, PA: Perseus Books Group.

———. (2003). *Managing Transitions,* 2d edition. Cambridge, MA: Da Capo Press.

Carnegie, D. (1936). *How to Win Friends and Influence People.* New York: Simon and Schuster.

Gladwell, M. (2002). *The Tipping Point: How Little Things Can Make a Big Difference.* New York: Back Bay Books/Little, Brown and Company.

Harvey, D.F., and D.R. Brown. (1988). *An Experiential Approach to Organization Development,* 3d edition. Englewood Cliffs, NJ: Prentice Hall.

Schein, E.H. (1992). *Organizational Cultural and Leadership.* San Francisco: Jossey-Bass.

Weisbord, M.R. (1993). *Discovering Common Ground: How Future Search Conferences Bring People Together to Achieve Breakthrough Innovation, Empowerment, Shared Vision, and Collaborative Action.* San Francisco: Berrett-Koehler.

Whitney, D., and A. Trosten-Bloom. (2003). *The Power of Appreciative Inquiry.* San Francisco: Berrett-Koehler.

Websites

Cooperrider, D. (2002, February). Appreciative Inquiry Commons, http://ai.cwru.edu/practice/toolsPackDetail.cfm?cold=1170.

Additional Resources

Books

Here is a list of books that will help you build your OD library and learn the various practices and methods used by OD practitioners today.

Argyris, C., and D.A. Schön. (1996). *Organizational Learning II.* Reading, MA: Addison-Wesley.

Beckhard, R., and R.T. Harris. (1977). *Organizational Transitions: Managing Complex Change.* Reading, MA: Addison-Wesley.

Bennis, W.G. (1969). *Organization Development: Its Nature, Origins, and Prospects.* Reading, MA: Addison-Wesley.

Berger, P.L., and T. Luckman. (1966). *The Social Construction of Reality.* New York: Anchor Books.

Block, P. (1999). *Flawless Consulting: A Guide to Getting Your Expertise Used.* San Francisco: Pfeiffer.

Boone, L.E., and D.D. Bowen. (1987). *The Great Writings in Management and Organizational Behavior,* 2d edition. New York: McGraw-Hill.

Bridges, J., and F.D. Peat. (1989). *Turbulent Mirror.* New York: Harper & Row.

Burke, W.W. (1982). *Organization Development Principles and Practices.* Boston: Little, Brown.

Burr, V. (1995). *An Introduction to Social Construction.* London: Routledge.

Byham, C., A. Smith, and M. Paese. (2002). *Grow Your Own Leaders: How to Identify, Develop, and Retain Leadership Talent.* Saddle River, NJ: Financial Times Prentice Hall.

Charan, R., S. Drotter, and J. Noel. (2000). *The Leadership Pipeline: How to Build the Leadership Powered Company.* San Francisco: Jossey-Bass.

Chawla, S., and J. Renesch, editors. (1995). *Learning Organizations: Developing Cultures for Tomorrow's Workplace.* Portland, OR: Productivity Press.

Cooperrider, D., D. Whitney, and J. Stavros. (2003). *Appreciative Inquiry Handbook: The First in a Series of AI Workbooks for Leaders of Change.* Brunswick, OH: Lakeshore Communications.

Davis, S.M., and P.R. Lawrence. (1977). *Matrix.* Reading, MA: Addison-Wesley.

French, W.L., and C.H. Bell, Jr. (1978). *Organization Development,* 2d edition. Englewood Cliffs, NJ: Prentice Hall.

French, W.L., C.H. Bell, Jr., and R.A. Zawacki, editors. (1978). *Organization Development and Transition,* 4th edition. Chicago: Irwin.

Gergen, K.J. (1999). *An Invitation to Social Construction.* London: Sage Publications.

Goldsmith, M., L. Lyons, and A. Freas. (2000). *Coaching for Leadership: How the World's Greatest Coaches Help Leaders Learn.* San Francisco: Pfeiffer.

Greiner, L.E., and V.E. Schein. (1989). *Power and Organization Development.* Reading, MA: Addison-Wesley.

Hall, R.H. (1987). *Organizations,* 4th edition. Englewood Cliffs, NJ: Prentice Hall.

Hampden-Turner, C., and F. Trompenaars. (1997). *Riding The Waves of Culture: Understanding Diversity in Global Business.* New York: McGraw-Hill.

Hargrove, R. (1995). *Masterful Coaching.* San Francisco: Pfeiffer.

Johnson, D.W., and F.P. Johnson. (2000). *Joining Together,* 7th edition. Boston: Allyn and Bacon.

Kinlaw, D. (1996). *Facilitation Skills: The ASTD Trainer's Sourcebook.* New York: McGraw Hill.

Lawler, E.W., III. (1983). *Pay and Organization Development.* Reading, MA: Addison-Wesley.

Leonard, T.J. (1998). *The Portable Coach.* New York: Scribner.

McGill, M.E. (1977). *Organization Development for Operating Managers.* New York: AMACOM.

Moore, C. (1992). *The Facilitator's Manual.* Chattanooga, TN: Chattanooga Venture.

Moss Kanter, R. (1985). *Change Masters.* New York: Free Press.

Owen, H. (1997). *Expanding Our Now: The Story of Open Space Technology.* San Francisco: Berrett-Koehler.

———. (1997). *Open Space Technology: A User's Guide.* San Francisco: Berrett-Koehler.

Owen, H., and A. Stadler. (2000). *Collaborating for Change: Open Space Technology.* San Francisco: Berrett-Koehler.

Rogers, C. (1995). *On Becoming a Person: A Therapist's View of Psychotherapy.* New York: Mariner Books.

Rothwell, W.J. (2000). *Effective Succession Planning: Ensuring Leadership Continuity and Building Talent From Within.* New York: American Management Association.

Rothwell, W.J., and R. Sullivan, editors. (2005). *Practicing Organization Development,* 2d edition. San Francisco: Pfeiffer.

Schein, E.H. (1999). *The Corporate Culture Survival Guide.* San Francisco: Jossey-Bass.

———. (1969). *Process Consultation: Its Role in Organization Development.* Reading, MA: Addison-Wesley.

Schwarz, R. (2002). *The Skilled Facilitator.* San Francisco: Jossey-Bass.

Seagal, S., and D. Horne. (1996). *Human Dynamics.* Waltham, MA: Pegasus Communications.

Senge, P.M., C. Roberts, R.B. Ross, B.J. Smith, and A. Kleiner. (1994). *The Fifth Discipline Fieldbook.* New York: Doubleday.

Shafritz, J.M., and J.S. Ott. (1987). *Classics of Organization Theory,* 2d edition. Chicago: The Dorsey Press.

Tubbs, S.L. (1995). *A Systems Approach to Small Group Interaction,* 5th edition. New York: McGraw-Hill.

Varney, G.H. (1977). *Organization Development for Managers.* Reading, MA: Addison-Wesley.

Weisbord, M.R. (1991). *Productive Workplaces.* San Francisco: Jossey-Bass.

Weisbord, M.R., and Janoff, S. (2000). *Future Search.* San Francisco: Berrett-Koehler.

Wheatley, M.J. (1992). *Leadership and the New Science.* San Francisco: Berrett-Koehler.

Whitney, D., D. Cooperrider, B. Kaplin, and A. Trosten-Bloom. (2001). *Encyclopedia of Positive Questions, Volume I: Using AI to Bring Out the Best in Your Organization.* Brunswick, OH: Lakeshore Communications.

Winer, M., and K. Ray. (1994). *Collaboration Handbook.* St. Paul, MN: Amherst H. Wilder Foundation.

Worley, C.G., D.E. Hitchin, and W.L. Ross. (1996). *Integrated Strategic Change.* Reading, MA: Addison-Wesley.

Organizations

Here is a list of organizations and Websites of interest to OD practitioners.

American Society for Training and Development. http://www.astd.org

Human Systems Dynamic Institute. http://www.hsdinstitute.org

International Coach Federation. http://www.coachfederation.org/default.asp

International Society for Performance Improvement. http://www.ispi.org

Organization Development Institute. http://members.aol.com/odinst

Organization Development Network. http://www.odnetwork.org

Organizational Dynamics Forum. http://finance.groups.yahoo.com/group/orgdyne

Society for Human Resources Management. http://www.shrm.org

Society for Industrial and Organizational Psychology. http://www.siop.org

About the Author

Lisa Haneberg has been an OD practitioner for 20 years. Her experience includes work for and with companies like Intel Corporation, Black & Decker, Mead Paper, Amazon.com, Beacon Hotel Corporation, Cruise West, and Travcoa. She is the author of *H.I.M.M. (High Impact Middle Management): Solutions for Today's Busy Managers* and numerous articles and e-books. Haneberg writes a management blog called *Management Craft* and regularly writes about OD topics. She has a bachelor's degree in behavioral sciences; completed graduate work in OD and human resources; attended professional training courses; and received certifications in the areas of facilitating, training, and behavioral tendencies assessment tools. Haneberg lives in Seattle, Washington, and has a consulting firm called Haneberg Management. For more information or to contact Lisa Haneberg, go to www .haneberg-management.com or write to her at lhaneberg@gmail.com.